Cool Britannia and Multi-Ethnic Britain

Cool Britannia and Multi-Ethnic Britain: Uncorking the Champagne Supernova attempts to move away from the melancholia of Cool Britannia and the discourse which often encases the period by repositioning this phenomenon through an ethnic minority perspective.

In March 1997, the front page of the magazine *Vanity Fair* announced 'London Swings! Again!' This headline was a direct reference to the swinging London of the 1960s – the English capital which became the era-defining epicentre of the world for its burgeoning rock and pop music scene, with its daring new youth culture, and the boutique fashion houses of Carnaby Street captured most indelibly by the Mods, Rockers, and psychedelic hippies of the time. In the 1990s this renewed interest in the swinging 60s seemed to reinvigorate popular culture, after a global period in the 1980s which would see the collapse of traditional communism and the ending of Cold War, while ushering in the beginnings of a new technological age spearheaded by Apple, Microsoft, and IBM. The dawn of the 1990s meant that peace and love would once again reign supreme, with Britannia being at the forefront of 'cool' again. Godfathers of the Mancunian Rock scene New Order would declare 'Love had the world in motion' and, for a fleeting period, Britain was about to encounter its second coming as the cultural epicentre of the world.

Although history proffers a period of utopia, inclusion, and cultural integration, the narrative alters considerably when exploring this euphoric period through a discriminatory and racialised lens. This book repositions the ethnic minority–lived experience during the 1990s from the societal and political margins to the centre. The lexicon explored attempts to provide an altogether different discourse that allows us to reflect on seminal and racially discriminatory episodes during the 1990s that subsequently illuminated the systemic racism sustained by the state. The Cool Britannia years become a metaphoric reference point for presenting a Britain that was culturally splintered in many ways. This book utilises storytelling and auto-ethnography as an instrument to unpack the historical amnesia that ensues when unpacking the racialised plights of the time.

Jason Arday is an Assistant Professor in Sociology in the Department of Sociology at Durham University.

Routledge Research in Race and Ethnicity

Cool Britannia and Multi-Ethnic Britain

Uncorking the Champagne Supernova

Jason Arday

Routledge
Taylor & Francis Group

LONDON AND NEW YORK

First published 2020
by Routledge
2 Park Square, Milton Park, Abingdon, Oxon OX14 4RN

and by Routledge
52 Vanderbilt Avenue, New York, NY 10017

Routledge is an imprint of the Taylor & Francis Group, an informa business

British Library Cataloguing-in-Publication Data
A catalogue record for this book is available from the British Library

Library of Congress Cataloging-in-Publication Data
Names: Arday, Jason, author.
Title: Cool Britannia and multi-ethnic Britain : uncorking the
    champagne supernova / Jason Arday.
Description: Abingdon, Oxon ; New York, NY : Routledge, 2020. |
    Includes bibliographical references and index.
Identifiers: LCCN 2019034556 (print) | LCCN 2019034557 (ebook) |
    ISBN 9781138217409 (hardback) | ISBN 9781315440644 (ebook)
Subjects: LCSH: Minorities—Great Britain—Social conditions. |
    Great Britain—Ethnic relations—History—20th century. |
    Great Britain—Race relations—History—20th century.
Classification: LCC DA125.A1 A855 2020 (print) |
    LCC DA125.A1 (ebook) | DDC 305.800941—dc23
LC record available at https://lccn.loc.gov/2019034556
LC ebook record available at https://lccn.loc.gov/2019034557

ISBN: 978-1-138-21740-9 (hbk)
ISBN: 978-1-315-44064-4 (ebk)

Typeset in Times New Roman
by Apex CoVantage, LLC

MIX
Paper from
responsible sources
FSC   FSC™ C013985
www.fsc.org

Printed in the United Kingdom
by Henry Ling Limited

Contents

Acknowledgements

It was my dream to write a book on a period that would ultimately define my life and that of countless others in many ways. The Cool Britannia years provided a soundtrack to my life that still reverberates in my ears today and that reverberation has made it possible to write this book.

I would like to thank the following colleagues and friends who have been instrumental in supporting me throughout this process: Heidi Mirza, Vikki Boliver, Michael Cobden, Melissa Clarke, Dave Thomas, Suhraiya Jivraj, Paul Warmington, Robbie Shilliam, Paulette Williams, Chantelle Lewis, Remi Joseph-Salisbury, Vini Lander, Dominik Jackson-Cole, Tamanda Walker, Marcia Wilson, Anthony Maher, Michael Hobson, Shirin Housee, Leah Bassel, Paul Miller, Shirley-Anne Tate, Delayna Spencer, Beth Thomas-Hancock, and Dina Belluigi. I also wish to thank the Routledge Editorial Team – Elena Chiu, Emily Briggs, Chris Mathews, and Lakshita Joshi – for their continued help. They have been unstinting in their support and patience on this important project.

I would like to extend a huge thanks to my exceptional family: Debbie-Ann, Taylah, Noah, Mum, Dad, Simon, and Joseph. As always, I would also like to extend my appreciation and gratitude to Sandro Sandri; without him . . . the dream would not possible.

To all the participants that participated in the initial early phase of this project some years ago: thank you so much for your stories of navigating racism throughout the 90s as an ethnic minority in

Britain. I only hope that I have been able to do your stories justice. This book would never have come to fruition if not for all of you; I am eternally grateful.

This book is dedicated to the enduring memory of Stephen Lawrence and his parents, Doreen and Neville, who have been unrelenting in their pursuit for racial equality in Britain. We all owe your family a significant debt of gratitude.

About the author

Dr Jason Arday is an Assistant Professor in Sociology at Durham University in the Department of Sociology. Jason is a Visiting Research Fellow at The Ohio State University in the Office of Diversity and Inclusion, a Research Associate at Nelson Mandela University in the Centre for Critical Studies in Higher Education Transformation and a Trustee of the Runnymede Trust, the UK's leading Race Equality Thinktank. Jason sits on the Centre for Labour and Social Studies (CLASS) National Advisory Panel and is a School Governor at Shaftesbury Park Primary School in London.

Jason also sits on the following trade union equality committees; Trade Union Congress (TUC) Race Relations Committee; University and College Union (UCU) Black Members' Standing Committee and the UK Council for Graduate Education (UKCGE) Working Group on BME Participation in Postgraduate Research. Jason is also part of the Universities UK Advisory Group on tackling racial harassment in higher education. He is a Graduate of the Operation Black Vote (OBV) MP Parliamentary Scheme, a scheme focused on unearthing the next generation of ethnic minority Parliamentarians.

Jason is author of the following titles: *Considering Racialized Contexts in Education: Using Reflective Practice and Peer-Mentoring to Support Black and Ethnic Minority Educators* (Routledge) and *Being Young, Black and Male: Challenging the Dominant Discourse* (Palgrave). He is the co-editor of the highly acclaimed *Dismantling*

Race in Higher Education: Racism, Whiteness and Decolonising the Academy (Palgrave) with Professor Heidi Mirza (Goldsmiths, University of London). Jason also serves on the Editorial Board of *Educational Philosophy and Theory* and speaks regularly at national and international conferences, as well as public and community events.

I am he as you are (s)he as you are me . . . and we are all together.

('I Am the Walrus', The Beatles, 1967)

Preface

There we were . . . now here we are . . .

This book is about multi-ethnic Britain, Cool Britannia, and institutional racism. This book attempts to move away from the melancholia of Cool Britannia and the discourse which often surrounds the period by repositioning this phenomenon through an ethnic minority perspective. Although history proffers a period of utopia, inclusion, and cultural integration, the narrative alters considerably when exploring this euphoric period through a discriminatory and racialised lens. In this book, ethnic minorities have been repositioned from the societal and political margins to the centre. The lexicon explored attempts to provide an altogether different discourse that allows us to reflect on seminal and racially discriminatory episodes during the 1990s that subsequently illuminated the systemic racism sponsored and sustained by the state. The term 'institutional racism' would come of age towards the end of 1990s, providing a societal and conceptual framework for understanding the perniciousness and centrality of racial discrimination in Britain.

In *Cool Britannia and Multi-Ethnic Britain: Uncorking the Champagne Supernova*, the Black and ethnic minority struggle during this period became collateral damage in an attempt to redefine the conception of 'Britishness' which had historically been narrow in definition and exclusive of a multi-cultural diverse diaspora. The Cool Britannia years become a metaphoric reference point for presenting a

Britain that was culturally splintered in many ways. My hope for this book is to use storytelling and auto-ethnography as an instrument to unpack an historical amnesia that conveniently overlooks the racialised plights of the time.

The dominant discourse has traditionally leant more in favour of a more playful, unencumbered soundtrack which positions the 90s as an inclusive and embracive period that was tolerant of communal and societal difference. On the contrary, the contexts presented throughout this book reflect something entirely different that illuminates the eternal struggle for racial equality against the tragic and enduring backdrop of the racially motivated murder of an 18-year-old aspiring architect from South London in 1993. This act of pure wickedness and the racism that would proceed this incident resulted in the Metropolitan Police Service (MPS) being declared by Sir William Macpherson as institutionally racist. This would become one of the most important moments in the modern history of criminal justice in Britain.

It is my sincere hope that this book will facilitate a reflection beyond what has become immortalised in British folklore as a period that was inspired by 60s pop culture and infused by youthful exuberance. There is a recognition that for many the Cool Britannia years evoke memories of a time in which there was an increased sense of pride in the culture of the United Kingdom, which subsequently sparked a renewed sense of optimism following the tumultuous years of the 1970s and 1980s. This celebration in 'British' culture must also acknowledge the plight of the marginalised and the racialised tensions of the time that created a hostile environment which resulted in ethnic minorities residing on the periphery of an institutionally racist society.

In confronting this issue, there will be an uncomfortable discourse for melancholic Britain to digest. The detanglement of this filtered portrayal attempts to eclipse the one often proffered when eulogising the 90s. Engaging in this way requires an orientation towards dismantling the notion that we resided in a national community that that prided itself on the principles of openness and tolerance while stealthily enacting the opposite, capably aided by the state. If this book modestly detangles part of this fallacy, then we can attempt to provide a more accurate and unfiltered narration of Britain's racialised history during the 1990s.

Abbreviations

Metropolitan Police Service (MPS)
Social Exclusion Unit (SEU)
United Kingdom (UK)
United States (US)
Women Against Fundamentalism (WAF)

A soundtrack to the book

Lightening Seeds: Lucky You
Tasmin Archer: Sleeping Satellite
The Verve: Sonnet
Oasis: Slide Away
Skunk Anansie: Hedonism
The Stone Roses: Ten Storey Love Song
Blur: This is a Low
New Order: World in Motion
Paul Weller: Out of the Sinking
New Radicals: You Only Get What You Give
Fatboy Slim: Praise You
Dodgy: In a Room
The Charlatans: The Only One I Know
Seal: Crazy
Cornershop: Brimful of Asha
The Cranberries: Dreams

Introduction

How people reflect on and recount a period of time is really interesting

In March 1997, the front page of the magazine *Vanity Fair* announced 'London Swings! Again!' This headline was a direct reference to the kaleidoscopic, colourful, swinging London of the 1960s – the English capital which became the era-defining epicentre of the world for its burgeoning rock and pop music scene, with its daring new youth culture, and the boutique fashion houses of Carnaby Street captured most indelibly by the Mods, Rockers, and psychedelic hippies of the time. In the 1990s, this renewed interest in the swinging 60s seemed to reinvigorate popular culture after a global period in the 1980s which saw the collapse of traditional communism and the ending of Cold War, while ushering in the beginnings of a new technological age spearheaded by Apple, Microsoft, and IBM. The dawn of the 1990s meant that peace and love would reign supreme once again; with Britannia being at the forefront of 'cool' again. Godfathers of the Mancunian Rock scene New Order would declare 'Love had the world in motion' and, for a fleeting period, Britain was about to encounter its second coming as the cultural epicentre of the world.

There are periods historically which capture the mood of a generation and become the soundtrack to a particular type of lived experience. The 1990s encapsulated a period of turbulence and euphoria with which individuals identified in various ways. Primarily, the fault of Thatcher's Conservative Government, British society was splintered with unrealistic notions of meritocracy and a system that did little to foster egalitarianism, invariably causing social, economic, and political unrest nationwide. During their tenure, the Conservatives managed to widen the chasm between the working class and middle class and between the rich and poor, creating further divisions and inequity. The lacerations inflicted by nearly two decades of Conservative rule were to be balm by a 'socialist cavalry' which represented a new cosmopolitan generation of parliamentarians, promising a new brand of politics. This was to be spearheaded and fronted by Labour centrist firebrand Tony Blair. The mid-1990s would give rise to the rebirth of a political machine that had resided in the political doldrums for nearly 20 years. This rejuvenated contemporary machine would be christened 'New Labour'. A renewed and strengthened sense of national pride propelled a wave of populism which reached fever pitch following the exploits of England National Football Team at the 1996 European Championships, where Britain collectively proclaimed that Football had returned to its spiritual home. The culmination of such a period, as often is the case within the media, required a punchy and definitive footnote to capture the moment and immortalise this period of time. The dismantling of almost 20 years of Conservative oppression, leading up to the crowning of the Labour Party as custodians of the British Government, proved to be the dawning of a period categorised as the 'Cool Britannia years'. The importance attributed to feelings that accompany significant periods in history often become immersed contextually within feelings, emotions, and experiences that allow one to reminisce about yesteryear.

Significant periods in most individuals' lives prove to be a point of discovery which can often lead to a sense of belonging that is hard to quantify. Conversely, a sense of exclusion or marginalisation can become apparent to individuals, where societal inclusivity can feel peripheral to a particular group of excluded individuals. The collective, or 'being a part of this', becomes an important vehicle for the contexts to be explored within this book because it is impossible to romantically reminisce about such a period without acknowledging that this particular episode in time was punctuated by some pertinent and historically defining events which ultimately culminated in the proffering of the Macpherson Report in 1999. The report illuminated what was probably one of the most known knowns – at least to people of colour within these shores – that Britain as a society was institutionally racist. Poignantly, it is against this backdrop that it is worth considering the juxtaposition of such a definitive period in British history. The euphoria that kept so many aloft throughout the decade regarding the renewed sense of optimism that proceeded a period of hostile oppressive rule under a Conservative government during the Thatcher years reflects something entirely different for ethnic minorities residing within a wasteland of racial discrimination. The rose-tinted glasses of an era which embraced the blinding populist sunshine, contrastingly, could not provide shelter or refuge to the ever-present darkening shadow of pernicious and insidious racism that had historically and consistently blighted British society. Only matched globally, and perhaps more overtly, through one of the most divisive and oppressive regimes of the 19th century: Apartheid in South Africa. The debilitating racial segregation in South Africa significantly shaped and set the tone for racial inequality globally, as this atrocity became apparent to the rest of the free world amidst an international campaign of isolation that resulted in a cultural boycott. This resistance and display of global solidarity affected all aspects concerning political, economic, cultural, and sporting representation regarding South Africa. The combination of concerted domestic, global, and political pressure would see the unconditional release of Nelson Rolihlahla Mandela in 1990 to an adoring South African Republic and the entire world after 27 years of imprisonment, hand in hand with Winnie Madikizela-Mandela, who for nearly three decades sustained and led the struggle for Black liberation and emancipation during Mandela's incarceration.

There is a personal resonance that depicts this period for me as the author, which resembles an auto-ethnographic and perhaps semi-biographical experience. This was very much a period of self-discovery in which I became very aware of the racial binaries that restricted taste and preference whilst reinforcing discriminatory and exclusionary cultures. The experience of traversing adolescence and my teenage years through that period provided an awakening regarding some of the tensions that underpinned British society at the time. Part of this enlightenment caused me to gravitate towards a band from Burnage, Manchester, who emerged from the Madchester music scene that dominated British popular culture at the time: Oasis. Upon purchasing my first album, *Definitely Maybe* by Oasis, this unearthed something which resonated with the social deprivation I encountered daily, growing up on a council estate and being from a working-class background. Subsequently, this provided the soundtrack to my teenage years. Upon reflection, there has often been a questioning of what in particular about this band struck a chord with me and I continue to wonder about it now, many years later. Perhaps it was the charged and frenetic aggression of the opening chords to the uncompromising 'Cigarettes and Alcohol', 'dubiously borrowed' from psychedelic and glam rock protagonists T. Rex, stating 'is it my imagination . . . or have I finally found something worth living for?' Or maybe it is the tale of four Mancunian working-class boys taking on the world and coming out on top. In any case, a spark was ignited and it provided something to aspire to that was situated within the British context; that perhaps a working-class South Londoner could take on the world and come out on top too – or at least so it seemed until the veil of naïveté and innocence was institutionally stripped away through the most pernicious and insidious of discriminatory instruments . . . racism.

In attempting to explain a story of inclusion and exclusion, my story very much resembled an anecdote of inclusion until my veil of naïveté and innocence was abruptly removed and my blissful awakening rudely interrupted when I was apprehended by the police as a 14-year-old, for what one can only recall was breathing. Typically, the opening gambit of the conversation began with 'you fit the description of . . .' The familiarity of this reference particularly to young Black males would provide an anecdote of systematic and racialised persecution. The fluidity of such discrimination remains an anchor for racial ascription, victimisation, and institutional racism within the United Kingdom.

The first encounter with the police was a significant experience, as it has been for many people of colour within the UK, and although forewarnings had been provided by those possessing the residual scarring of racialisation by the state, this would provide no preparation for the feelings of shame, vulnerability, helplessness, and injustice that would swiftly proceed my 'stop and search' encounter. Before this experience, I was totally engrossed and immersed within this anecdote of 'inclusion' which came in the form of the Cool Britannia machine and have often reflected upon what this meant for others; particularly multi-ethnic Britain and the stories and experiences of exclusion and marginalisation that permeated those individuals' existence during a particularly tense racial and discriminatory period.

The longevity of this inequality provides an enduring backdrop to how freely inequality pervades within British society, particularly when the plight of ethnic minority individuals is considered. The prevailing discourse of discrimination and marginalisation derives from the opportunity to detail some of racialised plights encountered by ethnic minorities through a societal, historical, and political lens that encapsulates the hedonism and divisiveness of the 1990s. As Paul Gilroy states in *There Ain't No Black in the Union Jack*, we are still a long way from comprehending why Britain has shown itself to be incapable of coming to terms with its Black and other minority settlers. This incapability to accept and be more receptive to difference provides the platform for exclusion and marginalisation in all of its discriminatory manifestations within society, whether this transpires in overt or covert forms. The egalitarian ideals that accompany inclusivity require us to continually challenge the notion of what this concept means, particularly within a British society that historically has been resistant to accepting and embracing difference. The potential inclusion or exclusion of multi-ethnic Britain during the Cool Britannia years against the dominant rhetoric of populism and patriotism is one that requires further exploration in attempting to understand how ethnic minorities perceived and reflect on this particular period. Thus, reflection becomes a powerful instrument for building a conceptual understanding of a lived experience. This instrument is pertinent in providing a voice to those on the periphery who remain marginalised by attempting to portray personal and collective interpretations of the inequitable cultural and societal dialogue that transpired during this racially turbulent but conversely euphoric period.

This book aims to illustrate that although Cool Britannia may have been regarded as a cultural phenomenon, mapped against an institutionally racist British society at the time, this euphoric period became exclusionary and would become weaponised to demonstrate disgruntlement at ethnic minorities residing in Britain. Uncorking this phenomenon will invariably cause some discomfort, but there is a need to develop a narrative that focuses upon the understudied and often marginalised histories of Black and ethnic minority Britons. The period to be explored resides in the duality of optimism and pessimism – primarily because the time in question also became an instrument for racial discrimination, fascism, and xenophobic endeavours which subsequently created a hostile and exclusionary environment. The arguments presented in this book will attempt to explore the impact of politics on racial inequality at the time constructed through three pertinent incidences: the murder of Stephen Lawrence in 1993, the induction of Tony Blair's New Labour Government in 1997, and the Macpherson Inquiry in 1997, which subsequently resulted in his report in 1999.

1 Love spreads

The impact of the Cool Britannia years on multi-ethnic Britain

Introduction

Too often it is assumed that Britain is and has always been an inclusive space, tolerant of all ethnic difference. The vernacular used to describe or define this inclusion is interesting, as the term becomes consumed in whichever applicable rhetoric or discourse suits the narrative at the time. This term has also been conferred to suggest that Black communities are problems to be theorised by White intellectuals, consequently placing ethnic minorities on the periphery of British society, unable to verbalise their experiences of residing in Britain as a minority (Warmington, 2014). The cost to this neglect is the portrayal of a phenomenon that is not entirely inclusive or accurate, resulting in an historical amnesia that ensues when reciting and extolling the virtues of the politically turbulent and drug-fuelled excess of the 90s. What this book attempts to do is reposition the narrative by utilising an auto-ethnographic approach to centre the voices of ethnic minorities during this period in understanding how the environment, the state, and its major institutions at the time were complicit in sustaining a racist, exclusionary, and discriminatory hostile environment.

Cool Britannia and Multi-Ethnic Britain: Uncorking the Champagne Supernova offers a story of how racism unfolded in the 1990s against the backdrop of Cool Britannia. Its focus attempts to dispel the myth that this period was inclusive of all British residents at the time. This book explores how ethnic minorities circumnavigated the landmines of racism throughout the decade by examining the resistance movements of the time and the impact of political discourse on this context. This introductory chapter begins by providing a biographical outline of the time which situates myself as the author, oscillating between the paradigms of inclusion and exclusion regarding the Cool Britannia phenomenon. Considerations within the chapter then move to the advent of New Labour and the subsequent impact on multi-ethnic Britain. This chapter positions the ethnic minority discriminatory plight regarding inclusion, exclusion, and marginalisation, providing the stimulus for further considerations of race and racism, belonging, cultural diversity, and integration throughout this book.

The revival of everything synonymous with eclectic Britain during the 1960s, when the nation held the world's attention for a period as the epicentre for music, fashion, culture, and sport, was reincarnated in the form of the Cool Britannia years which occupied a period during the mid-1990s. The essence of this period impacted several facets of society which are now engrained within British folklore and history. Integral to this sense of renewed optimism was a feeling of psychedelia and euphoria, a sense of freedom and expression that was perceived to have been suppressed under oppressive Conservative rule. Built upon a wave of hope and optimism, there is a narrative that provides a counter to this melancholia. The counternarrative reflects a different type of oppression which was systemic and insidious throughout the period following the nationalist revival in the 1980s, in which the shackles of subjugation remained and the right of emancipation denied. This decade observed an uprising, in which victimised and racialised multi-ethnic individuals within Britain began to 'visibly' challenge the inequity they encountered with a sustained resistance through anti-racist activism and a new breed of civil rights politics which directly challenged the normative orthodoxy and inherent fluidity of discrimination, principally racial discrimination. A brief historical interjection saw the release of anti-Apartheid revolutionary and Nobel Peace Prize laureate Nelson Mandela at the beginning of the 1990s after 27 years of imprisonment, after being convicted of attempting to overthrow the state following the Rivonia Trial. However, this did not quell the continuation of institutional racism faced by Black and ethnic minority individuals nationally within the UK or globally. Often this narrative is submerged within the Cool Britannia years which further highlights how particular factions of society during that period of time operated on the periphery of this cultural phenomenon, thus creating a powerful anecdote for inclusion and exclusion and, perhaps more significantly, which types of individuals are able to access this type of 'belonging'.

The importance of such a period is encapsulated in the eyes of those who experienced this particular phenomenon; this becomes a central theme within this book. The prevailing discourse becomes integral in attempting to challenge the romance of a period which often situates its rhetoric within an inclusive paradigm. The turbulence of this period is punctuated by particular landmark events; within a racialised context there are two significant historical milestones which illuminated the plight of institutional racism within all its forms. The murder of Stephen Lawrence became a yardstick for measuring how insidiously racism was saturated throughout the fabric of British society. The MacPherson Report brought to the British public's attention the depths of this discriminatory saturation and how it pervaded all of Britain's major institutions. Importantly, it highlighted the impact of this discriminatory terrain on Black and ethnic minority communities throughout the UK.

This compelling counternarrative is one that often is lost within the rhetoric of the time. The anecdote often proffered regarding the period often symbolises a tale of hope and optimism, which coincides with the resurgence of Britannia at the epicentre of postmodernism. The melancholy and psychedelia which accompanied this period is best typified through The Stone Roses' mantra of 'Love Spreading', a historical and cultural period within Britain that can only be rivalled by the swinging 60s. For Ian Brown and his brothers-in-arms, this mantra would become immortalised at the legendary Spike Island concert in May 1990. This gathering became an enduring symbol of what societal harmony and unity could look like . . . albeit against a backdrop of semi-psychedelic guitar-based riffs, bewitching melodies, and beatific, bass-laden funk grooves. This opening gambit provides an introductory context considering some of the more definitive nuances of the Cool Britannia years, in addition to exploring some of the features which captivated and generated global interest as Britain became the front-runner in popular culture, music, politics, and the arts. The consideration of this period also lends itself to a biographical account of how this particular period impacted a young Black male teenager from South London, in what essentially became a definitive, life-changing period that would become the catalyst for self-discovery.

Being a young black teenager during the Cool Britannia years

This tale initially is framed within an 'inclusive' context during a period of self-discovery. Binaries across the spectrum of intersectionality can sometimes become an interesting anchor towards engagement and expression; they ascribe individuals to a perceived societal narrative which often reflects some type of stereotype or racial ascription (Alleyne, 2002). This is something I became very aware of as a teenager who was heavily into guitar and rock music and who was a Black person – I was continuously reminded, through overt barbs and thinly veiled microaggressions, that as a person from my ethnic background, 'you should not really be into this type of thing', swiftly followed by references of Bounty (a term which denotes a Black person as Black on the outside and White on the inside). I remember the first time being labelled with this derogatory term and the feeling of helplessness and vulnerability that accompanied my bemusement, as I had been unaware that there was a blueprint, or a set of ascribed characteristics, for being 'Black'. Stunned into silence, I was completely taken aback. Interestingly, there was a period of awakening which also embraced the idea that, as a young Black male, I refused to assimilate into the 'perceived' stereotype but rather chose to be true to myself and what defined me as an individual, acutely aware that my interests in a particular genre of music and popular culture would situate me in predominantly White domains and spaces, where

I would become aware that I was the 'other' or was encountering 'othering'.

There is often a catalyst for something that ignites a particular interest. The ignition of this interest is maintained through social dynamics situated within how one identifies with certain types of social capital (Bygott, 1992; Warmington, 2014). As a teenager during this period, I was fortunate to have parents that made me politically conscious of the racialised plights facing people of colour around the world. This particular political compass was carefully navigated throughout my teenage years by parents who continuously made me and my siblings aware that there were several pitfalls and injustices that could be encountered being a young Black man within the global society, and my parents frequently cited examples of this being nowhere more prevalent than in the UK and the United States. What begins to be captured in this narrative growing up is effectively a survival toolkit for how to navigate residence within a racist society that often places people of colour on the periphery of opportunity, equality, and equity. By this point, the idea of inclusion seems a distant feature, whereby the rules for participation are facilitated by particular types of individuals with the power and the privilege to reinforce and perpetuate a cycle of inequality that has been built by historically excluding a particular demographic of individuals.

The topography of this exclusion is one that perhaps I was not privy to as I entered my teenage years immersed within the vacuum of Cool Britannia. During that particular period an obsession grew with a movement that seemed to be challenging the hierarchal and normative Conservative orthodoxy which had prevailed for several decades, disadvantaging many within British society. The antithesis to this orthodoxy was represented by a group of White working-class Mancunians, who would leave an indelible mark on British popular music: Oasis. The story of inclusion emerges when feelings of similarity and familiarity are bound within the context of the music, the sharing of a common language, which ultimately creates a form of tribalism (Harris, 2004). However, entry into the tribe and establishing the terms for belonging become very dependent upon a set of variables that are racialised and exclusionary. This becomes apparent in attempting to understand and decipher the societal construct which surrounds me and why people are resistance to my 'obvious difference' in comparison with them. As the music of the band began to take on a different meaning to me, with particular regards to how I conceptualised the world that surrounded me, I found myself often and upon reflection quite naïvely removing the context of 'race' and 'racism' from this interest.

On reflection, there is an acknowledgement that this may have been an avoidance mechanism situated in denial that 'race' and 'racism' could not impact such contexts as the communal and collective enjoyment derived from music. Interestingly, this becomes quite a pivotal moment, as a cognition transpires which ignites a political consciousness that potentially this type of music, while enjoyable, did not necessarily speak to my lived and future racialised experiences, particularly because a racialisation occurred in those predominantly White spaces which positioned me as a space invader, an outsider, a traveller absent direction, accidentally ending up in the wrong location. In a way, perhaps my own thinking was restricted and confined to thinking that, as a Black person, I did not belong in those spaces. Although the music acted as a form of escapism, this did not remove me from the physical and emotional reality of racial discrimination, with continual reiterations of this discriminatory instrument reminding me that, as a young Black male, I should not be gaining influence from this particular genre of music, as it had no correlation to being an oppressed person of colour within British society. Intriguingly, and perhaps conversely, this was something that I was actually reminded of by people of colour and White people of a similar age to me at the time. The internal conflict in relation to this context, therefore, becomes more intriguing when a reflection ensues regarding positionality within the story of inclusion and exclusion as an ethnic minority traversing adolescence in the 1990s. The resonance that accompanied the obsession with a band like Oasis affirmed my thoughts on iconic musical acts that had encapsulated a period of time; within this particular cultural period it became apparent that we were residing musically in a period during which we were in the presence of one of the definitive British bands of our time. Upon reflection, this internal affirmation may have been an attempt to integrate and assimilate myself into something that was different from the social and economic deprivation that I encountered daily.

Growing up on a council estate in South London, there were continual reminders of the path that individuals had trodden underpinned by a lack of opportunity to become socially mobile and remove themselves from the cyclical stranglehold of social deprivation, criminal activity, and gang affiliation. The blissfulness and naïveté that accompanies youth did not impair observations which queried and juxtaposed why certain types of individuals lived in a particular way while others lived in more affluent dwellings. Thus, the way in which one stimulates the mind with ideas associated with one day becoming socially mobile and removing oneself from abject poverty becomes an essential vehicle for mentally transporting from a particular situation towards envisaging a perfect utopia. The story of four working-class Mancunians who grew up with each other complimented this narrative for me. It provided an idealistic framework from which there was a feeling that 'racism' as a construct could be removed, and in its absence a more inclusive discourse could be espoused when situated within a class context. Effectively, this became quite a naïve and misinformed attempt to employ 'commonality' regarding the lived experience of racial discrimination. A cognition would later emerge which recognised that such factors are rarely inseparable for people of colour and in many ways are inescapable, particularly within a hostile environment. The premise for this cognition stems from an observational realisation which recognised a distinct difference in the way White and Black people are treated within society. This epiphany indicated that people of colour are rarely afforded the opportunity to become socially mobile, a construct underpinned by the inequitable anchor of institutional racism within society.

The process of identifying with these four individuals in Manchester became a cathartic process in attempting to digest and understand the world that was revolving around me at the time, and perhaps more pertinently, how individuals transpired within that world and how they were able to identify a sense of belonging to a particular movement or set of collective commonalities or circumstances. It also created distance from accepting the reality of living in a racist society, something I was reluctant to acknowledge in attempting to preserve the proverbial utopian bubble. Within this context, the commonalities reside within a narrative which fluctuates between being proud to be all things British and understanding how one begins to make sense of one's place within British society, and the implications which permeate the landscape of inclusivity, diversification, and ethnic tolerance. This consideration becomes even more significant when considering a country with a strained racial and oppressive past, a country within which there has been an historical intolerance towards multi-ethnicity and racial difference beyond that of the visual normative 'White' orthodoxy. The topography for race becomes even more apparent when considerations unpack how systematic racism operated during this period and how it became an oppressive instrument in victimising Black and ethnic minority individuals within Britain. Reflecting upon that first encounter with the police at the age of 14, a physical and mental impact ensued that invariably would spark a metacognition about society and its constructs. In particular, attention became drawn to the festering intolerance for multi-ethnic societies which coincided with an increase in the rise of populist and nationalist rhetoric. Though these affirmations and conceptions were drawn during the 1990s, it is safe to assert in many respects that the narrative of exclusion currently remains the same, albeit in more covert and sophisticated forms. One could perhaps assert that the potency of this exclusion has become more insidious, as racial intolerance towards ethnic difference becomes more prevalent and commonplace. Commonality amongst communities is now found in the resistance to embracing multi-ethnicity within Britain, a resistance which contradicts the notion of inclusivity and disrupts the concept of belonging and community, particularly within a British societal context. Commonality can also be found in the decisiveness or cohesiveness of politics, in which common ground can be gained or contested (Anderson, 1983). Wherever one's political allegiance may lie, a commonly shared treatise recognises that politics often play a pivotal part in determining the landscape of opportunity within society.

The impact of New Labour on multi-ethnic Britain

The advent of New Labour saw a merging of renewed hope, optimism, and the dawning of rock and roll politics propelled by the Britpop movement. A strategic and carefully mixed concoction of musical influence, political disfranchisement, and renewed generational optimism swept throughout Britain, as many relished the potential ending of nearly two decades of oppressive Conservative rule (Heffernan et al., 2016). For many of Britain's youth during this period, this dawning represented a seismic shift which promised better opportunities, greater access, and the opportunity for all members of society to become socially and economically mobile. In essence, the then-leader of the Labour Party, Tony Blair, attempted to deliver the most ambitious of ambitions to an already downtrodden majority of working-class and multi-ethnic Britons: a more equal society (Kenny, 2015). History dictates whether this objective was delivered to Labourites and society more generally; however, during this period there was a collective acknowledgement that the great British public would entertain just about any 'notion of hope' in anticipation of greater social mobility (Driver and Martell, 2006; Warmington, 2014). This also came via resistance to a previous Conservative regime that had widened the chasm of inequality and deprivation during its tenure at the helm of British politics. There is an argument to suggest that what makes politics distinctive at differing times throughout history is its interpretation of the current societal consensus, which invariably encompasses a difference of interests, beliefs, and value systems that embody contextually different perspectives, in attempting to help create and sustain commonality in values. The time that preceded the arrival of New Labour required a rethinking of the challenging economic and structural inequality that pervaded within factious Britain, particularly in the North of England. Conservatives will invariably argue that long-term social and economic trends such as industrialisation, secularisation, rationalisation, globalisation, and regionalisation shape the contexts and constraints within which all politicians have to operate, at times resulting in reduced opportunities to become socially mobile (Heffernan, 2001; Hindmoor, 2004). For socialists during the 1990s, the induction of New Labour represented a new vision for a more egalitarian Britain. The Blairite juggernaut was tasked with halting the inexorable force that was the Conservative Government. Identity politics became particularly pertinent as young people at the time began to frame their political orientation towards an ideal that embraced greater equity and opportunity for all, not just for a few (Hindmoor, 2004). At the time, Labour rather opportunistically attempted to provide a form of identity politics which helped to situate political and electoral nomads, with a focus on establishing strong links with the socially deprived and disenfranchised (Hitchens, 2004; Kymlicka, 1996).

Evangelising and presenting politics through the lens of identity allowed people to focus on who they were and where they belonged. Belonging and commonality were entrusted with party ideologies that represented thoughts, feelings, and lived experiences. This understanding for ethnic minorities in many ways assists in anchoring politics to a specific time and space; in other words, which political machine has done the most to elevate the burden of racialised and discriminatory oppression for this demographic? Individuals with a socialist disposition throughout society, including myself, would probably suggest Labour. Although perhaps an important interjection to make is that, generally, political orientation or affiliation will be purely subjective in conjecture which could easily be contested by those swayed to a more Conservative disposition. Whether swayed by either Labour or Conservative during the 1990s, there was a distinctive aspect of British politics which was and still is deeply entrenched in the notion of 'Britishness', rooted in the territorial politics of its multi-national state (Hall, 1998; Gilroy, 1993). For not the last time in this auto-ethnography, enter Britpop and the Cool Britannia years. Charged with a political agenda, Britpop was utilised as a vehicle to voice disgruntlement at the existing establishment, often proffering a socialist, liberal, and working class narrative situated in the arts and activist politics (Harris, 2004). There was a sense of opportunism exploited by politicians of the time, who were fully aware that the Britpop phenomenon cradled an aspiring generation of young people within the palm of its hand. The protagonists of the Britpop movement became aware of this and used their platform as a vehicle to illuminate social issues concerning the capitalist endeavour of the middle classes and the disillusionment of the working class. The prevailing narrative was spearheaded by Blur and Oasis, in particular Noel Gallagher, who famously attended a gathering of the great and good from the world of arts and culture, the best of the British, hosted by Blair at Number 10 Downing Street. Gallagher would narcissistically cite Blair's government and his band as the main catalysts for a societal revolution within in a somewhat fractured Britain at the time. Upon reflection, the comment itself smacked of self-indulgence and vanity bordering almost on a self-fulfilling prophecy, but such was the influence and gravitas of Britpop and British bands at the time that politicians recognised the significance of capitalising on this fad and aligning their political causes and ambitions to the British musicians who, by being in vogue, became the voice of modern youth culture (Harris, 2004).

The stature of these musicians meant that politicians were clamouring to enlist the support of these quintessential British performers effectively as governmental mules to endorse and spread the 'political gospel' in reference to particular political agendas or orientations. Tony Blair in particular would opportunistically hitch his wagon to the proverbial Britpop bougie, momentarily becoming cool by association. To some, this presented itself as another of example of politicians exploiting youth rebellion and disenfranchisement as a vehicle to pedal their own political agendas, manifestos, and careers. Interestingly, as these narratives become juxtaposed, it becomes difficult for ethnic minority individuals on the periphery of increased nationalism to discern where they fit within this populist landscape (Kundnani, 2007). This becomes pertinent during this period, primarily because there still remained a paucity of representation and diversification, particularly in positions of seniority and influence within the UK's major institutions. Further, feelings of displacement were exacerbated as the media begin to ignite and stamp their authority on the Britpop phenomenon by establishing a class war, famously pitting Noel Gallagher's Oasis against Damon Albarn's Blur. Oasis presented as the Northern working-class heroes and Blur presented as the Southern middle-class art school graduates. The proceeding narrative, however, was very much situated within a White, generally Male, and middle-class lexicon that omitted the voices of ethnic minorities who were placed on the margins through various institutionally racist structures (Farrar, 2004; Harris, 2004). Brief intermissions and disruptions to the racialised vernacular were provided by a modernised and reconceptulised version of feminism which spoke to empowering a 'new' young and fearless female generation: Girl Power. The Spice Girls represented something entirely different and were to some extent apolitical and more flexible in their approach towards politics which endorsed cross-party engagement, despite their endorsement of Thatcher as the 'first Spice Girl' and the pioneer of Girl Power. At the heart of their political interest was supporting a brand of politics that provided better outcomes for all citizens within British society. This was particularly intriguing given famous individuals' strong allegiances to party affiliations; such was the gravitas of politics at the time. Given the polarising nature of Thatcher, the Spice Girls did cause controversy at the time by citing the much-maligned and controversial former Conservative Prime Minster as the 'new leader of their band' (Harris, 2004). However, what did emerge from this proclamation was a point of reference in particular for young Black girls in observing a mixed-raced pop star in the form of Leeds native Melanie Brown, who became instantly identifiable with multi-ethnic Britain. This was powerful, given that at the time there were only a handful of visible, prominent Black people within the arts and culture industry within the UK.

This dearth of diversification outside of sport was palpable as typically dominant discourses situated Blacks as being proficient only in sport or in specific genres of music. In some ways this provided a somewhat small opening for ethnic minorities to engage in the festivities of Cool Britannia, despite having little visual and cultural stimulus prevalent in the media. The dearth of ethnic minority references in the UK within popular culture at that time painted a picture perhaps of a Britain that was not so culturally inclusive or diverse, unless you were part of the dominant White majority at the time. For me personally, there was an individual who managed to penetrate this ivory phenomenon and she represented something entirely different from the bubble-gum infused pop of the Spice Girls. This individual challenged the accepted, normative perception of the 'frontman' by the fact that she was a woman, but perhaps more importantly, she was a woman of colour which completely dismantled inherent, binary stereotypes about what was perceived as 'Black music'. This ignorance pervaded at a time in which Black musical interest was ignorantly confined to just 'gangster rap' which portrayed predominantly Black men glamourising violence and sexually objectifying women. An unsavoury trope which at the time was solely and exclusively levelled just at Black men, in this regard male patriarchy transcends racism and the objectification of women is a colour-blind endeavour. Her name was Deborah Anne Dyer was a trailblazer and a Black British person of Jamaican descent, better known by her stage name: Skin and frontwoman of Skunk Anansie. The band was one of the prominent groups that formed part of the Britrock movement which ran alongside Britpop. A South London native, the Brixtonian was able to cultivate a movement that broke conventions of stereotypical Black musical interest, in that she was an artistically expressive Black British woman who became a bona fide rock star who challenged the heteronormative orthodoxy and male patriarchy of Cool Britannia. In every way imaginable, Skin became a trailblazer during the Cool Britannia movement, in that she that was able to disrupt the overwhelmingly White and male-dominated stranglehold at the time. She became a visual focal point for ethnic minority alternative music enthusiasts to relate to, including myself. Skin was also able to dismantle conventions of White, European beauty with a gravitational aesthetic and androgyny that captivated the imaginations of rock music lovers, making her instantly recognisable and distinctive, adding to her effortless authenticity. Her presence would challenge the largely White Cool Britannia phenomenon by disrupting the 'conventional'. Her political activism as a staunch liberal became part of the groundswell during the 1990s in Britain for celebrated musicians to utilise their musical platforms to challenge inequality in all its forms and to create awareness around issues such as class, religion, disability, gender, sexuality, and, of course, racism within society.

The Britpop scene was a fantastic accompaniment to British politics at the time as politicians began to understand the impact of subcultures in helping to steer political agendas (Harris, 2004). Apart from anything else, this vehicle was utilised as an instrument for interest convergence in canvassing an expectant young generation scarred from the previous Tory administration. Conversely, the euphoria of this period also helped to conceal the insidious underbelly of Britain that operated on a system of deficiency, supremacist ideology, and discrimination which viewed ethnic minorities as inferior in many facets of society institutionally (Hall, 1998). The challenge for New Labour, and Blair in particular, was daunting. The wholesale change needed required a government that was going to concentrate its efforts entirely on destabilising the normative orthodoxy that had disadvantaged Black and ethnic minorities for decades, while attempting to advance a generational shift in attitudes, particularly among many White Britons who were the beneficiaries of the existing status quo (Bourne, 2001; Hindmoor, 2004).

There was a feeling that the advent of New Labour helped to place some of the racialised issues faced by ethnic minorities on the political agenda. In 1997, the New Labour Government – some may sceptically suggest in a bid to gain more of the ethnic minority electorate – were eager to affirm a commitment to social justice and racial equality, addressing long-standing educational grievances that had generationally disadvantaged people of colour (Gilroy, 2000; Warmington, 2014). However, overcoming and detangling an inequitable legacy left by the Tories was particularly difficult as Britain required a new conceptualisation of what a fairer and more equitable system could look like. There was a Conservative hangover for a period which led to the continuation of Conservative market policies which did little to improve diversity in schooling (Gillborn and Mirza, 2001; Heppell, 2014). In fact, a systematic targeting of 'failing' schools, which often had large numbers of ethnic minority pupils, deepened school segregation and racial inequality (Gillborn and Mirza, 2001). New Labour's commitment to creating a more socially just society was optimistically, if not a little hesitantly, applauded by multi-cultural Britain.

The prioritisation of race as a top-table agenda item was, until New Labour, quite frankly nonexistent. Perhaps the clearest indication regarding the trivialisation of race-related issues by the Conservative Government was between 1990 and 1997. Conservative fidelity towards antiracism policies from the 1970s to the mid-1990s were questionable, to say the least. Under Tory governance, issues concerning racial and ethnic inequality in education and society were virtually removed from political consideration, a failing acknowledged in 1997 by the outgoing Prime Minister John Major who suggested that policies must be colour blind, with a specific focus on tackling disadvantage before the installation of Blair's New Labour (Gillborn and Mirza, 2001). This thinly veiled admission regarding the need for future policies to address inequity and disadvantage by Britain's most prominent politician at the time was a watershed moment in providing something tangible for multi-cultural Britain to hang its withered hopes and aspirations on. Following election victory in 1997, New Labour was eager to affirm its view of a modern national identity which valued and endorsed cultural diversity in addition to recognising the citizenship rights of settled minorities and the inequalities that they faced (Gilroy, 2000; Neal, 2003).

During this period, Black and ethnic minorities began to observe a change in political focus which attempted to situate the Black vote as valued. Importantly, and perhaps quite strategically, Labour recognised the significance of having the majority of the UK Black electorate and the profitable impact of prioritising the needs of a group that had been systemically failed by successive governments (Farrar, 2004; Shukra, 1998). Blair knew this would be pivotal not only in extending his Premiership but also in ensuring that Labour remained at the helm of British politics for a considerable period of time (Gilroy, 2000; Phillips and Phillips, 1999). Endeavouring to – or being seen to – satisfy ethnic minority Britain would ultimately pay dividends in successive General Elections for Blair, who would serve as Prime Minster for ten years. There were many at the time who felt that the strategy employed was another example of political exploitation and shrewd interest convergence (Grasso, 2016). Actually, reflecting upon this there was enough evidence to suggest that Labour's mantra targeted at creating a fairer and just society was not merely rhetoric, the Party did task itself with initiating penetrative and targeted interventions aimed at tackling alarming disparities regarding inequality in Britain (Owusu, 2000). Within a year of its installation, despite being considered to be a vacuous, corporate, populist machine, New Labour had attempted to tackle a number of long-running societal grievances and inequalities (Hindmoor, 2004). This included the installation of the Social Exclusion Unit (SEU) which would enquire immediately into the issue of school exclusion and truancy, particularly relating to Black students (Bhopal and Maylor, 2014). New Labour's first White Paper illuminated inequalities in achievement by different ethnic groups and the lack of proper mentoring and support. The White Paper also proposed a replacement of the outdated Section 11 grant with an Ethnic Minorities Achievement Grant. This intervention became the catalyst to the decision to offer Muslim schools state funding similar to that given to existing Anglican, Catholic, Methodist, and Jewish schools (Ball, 2008; Housee, 2012). Further advancement in tackling racial and ethnic disparity would see Labour announce the setting up of an inquiry in the wake of the murder of Black student Stephen Lawrence in 1993 (MacPherson, 1999).

The story of inclusion, marginalisation, and exclusion for multi-ethnic Britain

Inclusion is an all-encompassing concept that embraces super-diversity across a spectrum of intersections such as race, ethnicity, culture, disability, sexuality, religion, and class (Sivanandan, 2006). What becomes interesting is when and how we apply this broad understanding of inclusivity and which individuals benefit from this conception. The advent of diversification is still something that provides a conundrum to varying sections of society, particularly for ethnic minorities who can sometimes struggle to fathom or hesitate to embrace this term as a catalyst for multi-culturalism and hyper-diversity (Shukra, 1998; Sivanandan, 1983). My personal understanding of the term has always been conflated within a narrative of being a son to second-generation African parents. Embracing the term then purely becomes a process of socialisation and cultural exposure . . . how do we as a society perceive diversity? For many Britons during the 1990s and beyond, this has become quite problematic against a perceived landscape of censorship regarding freedom of speech in favour of hyper-sensitivity and political correctness becoming exhausted (Warmington, 2013). Identity very much permeates this narrative because historically in Britain, we have resided within a society that has marginalised ethnic minorities, in most cases exploiting their physical and intellectual labour for commercial profit or economic gain. For many ethnic minorities, particularly those from migrant backgrounds who will often integrate themselves within British society utilising a form of intellectual or physical labour, there has been a populist resistance regarding the impact of their influence which has traditionally been couched within a nationalist and fascist rhetoric (Sivanandan, 2006; Song, 2003; St. Louis, 2007). What accompanies this is a feeling of conjecture and trepidation that normally poses ethnic minorities and individuals from migrant backgrounds as a threat towards employment, schooling, the economy, the welfare system and housing. My encounters with this narrative, as a young teenager transitioning into adulthood, encompassed a dialogue that always framed migrants as 'those people that come over here . . . steal our benefits and take our jobs'. Something regularly espoused to my parents and other migrant workers who have experienced this racially charged normative disenfranchisement by some White Britons. Despite being born in England, seldom was I ever shielded from or spared the impending questioning that commonly accompanies racialisation and migration discourse: 'where are you from?' to which I normally reply, 'England'. The question that then proceeds from this overtly prejudiced tête-à-tête concludes with the often inevitable and offensively predictable 'where are your parents from, you do not look English . . .?' For many second-generation British inhabitants, this is an all-too-familiar conversational interchange intertwined within a fascist and racist undertone.

Viewing this through the lens of the 1990s, sometimes an historical amnesia is applied which presents a temporary, harmonious return to the euphoria of the 1960s and swinging London. Ironically, this period also resided against a backdrop of cultural imperialism which asserted Britain as the dominant force in Western living society once again. The membership for cultural integration and entry often marginalised ethnic minority Britons, who historically and presently are still trying to traverse the institutionally racist terrain of Britain (Adi, 1995; Preston, 2010). The custodians of the dominant orthodoxy at this time were (among many others) the now defunct far-right fascist group National Front, which became politicised and modernised into the British National Party (BNP). Ideologically positioned on the far-right of the British political spectrum, the BNP's origins are firmly based in fascism and an enduring narrative which posits that only White people should reside as citizens within the UK (Shukra, 1998). Being on the periphery of any societal sanctum is difficult; it becomes even more difficult when inclusion within the sanctum is based on biological determinants in which most people do not have a say. Admittedly, eugenics has historically impacted this dialogue regarding notions of 'controlled breeding' and Aryan supremacy, resulting in attempts to ethnically cleanse, often at the expense of ethnic minorities (Ramdin, 1999; Rex and Tomlinson, 1979). The legacy of isolation, exclusion, and marginalisation for ethnic minorities resides in the ideology that Britain has longed for more stringent border controls which advance the end of non-White migration into the UK (Adi, 1995; Gilroy, 1992; Rex and Tomlinson, 1979). The clamour for such exclusion resides in a colonial and historical belief by hardened nationalists that all non-White Britons should be stripped of their citizenship and removed from British shores (Rose and Deakin, 1969; Robinson, 1983; Rush, 2002). Against a backdrop of deliverance, harmony, and serenity plagiarised from the 1960s, the 1990s became a renaissance for a liberated Britain, which became somewhat contradictory as dispositions for advancing notions associated with egalitarianism such as inclusion, multi-culturalism,

equity, and diversity were often in conflict with nationalist disposition and resistance to greater diversification within British society
(Adi, 1995; Solomos, 2003). The resounding calls for the removal of
non-White Britons throughout the 1990s provided a pernicious backdrop that subsequently placed ethnic minorities in positions of vulnerability, particularly in relation to the threat of violent, verbal, and
symbolic acts of racism. This 'backdrop' reminds us that although
the 1990s were heralded as the defining era that embodied hedonism,
lad-culture, music domination, and drug-fuelled excess as a patriotic
and enduring symbol of all things 'Cool Britannia', there remained
a group of individuals on the periphery of this definitive period who
did not experience and enjoy all the virtues of that period. The ethnic minority recital of this period is often punctuated by a sense of
not belonging, accompanied by feelings of negating dual cultures
in a desperate attempt to integrate and immerse oneself into British
culture as a method of survival, which has sometimes resulted in
compromising aspects of cultural identity (Pilkington, 2003; Rush,
2002). For many ethnic minorities this tends to be an 'unspoken sac-
rifice' which can often temporarily disconnect them with their own
cultural heritage against an all-too-familiar forced endorsement of
British imperialism which has traditionally involved pledging allegiance and faithfulness to the Queen, her heirs, and successors, and
by proxy her Empire, in reciting the oath required to obtain British
citizenship (Gilroy, 1992; Kundnani, 2007). The trade-off is difficult; essentially, most ethnic minority migrants enter the British Isles
for the promise of a better life and building something generational
within an economically well-developed country. However, in fulfill-
ing this vision, ethnic minorities often concede ground which sees
them suffer economically, physically, mentally, socially, and culturally. The type of capital conceded places ethnic minority migrant
workers in a particularly precarious and vulnerable position which
exposes them to greater risks of alienation, isolation, and marginalisation within adopted communities where migrant settlers often
reside in solitary capacities as the only people of colour, depending on which parts of Britain they move to geographically (Bygott,
1992; Miles, 1989).

**Understanding our story on screen: the impact
of Desmond's on the migrant narrative
throughout the 1990s**

Understanding the story of migration and integration into British
society for many ethnic minority families was best exemplified in
the ground-breaking Channel Four comedy *Desmond's*. The comedy
satire charts the experience of a first-generation West Indian family.
The family accurately represent the struggles of the time, particularly for the Windrush generation. Typically, until this point the characterisation of ethnic minorities, particularly on screen in Britain,
had been negative for a generation of Black children growing up
in the 1990s, which coincided with a dearth of diversification and
ethnic representation. Often, transatlantic offerings were accessed
to observe positive representations of Black people, most notably
Quincy Jones' American sitcom *The Fresh Prince of Bel-Air*, which
attempts to reposition the dominant vernacular concerning Black
people at the time as destitute, uneducated gang affiliates to edu-
cated, middle-class, and professionally successful. This became an
impressionable point of reference for many ethnic minority children
and adolescents within the UK who were beginning to have their
conceptions of Black people challenged in favour of a more positive
visual representation.

Desmond's was able to entice a generation that understood all
the perils associated with leaving the native comforts of home and
moving to completely unknown shores. The programme created a
synergy among ethnic minorities that achieved something truly special by demonstrating how the sanctuary of a barbershop became a
vehicle for social inclusion and integration. The situational comedy,
broadcast by Channel 4 from 1989 to 1994, was the brainchild of
Trix Worrell. The setting for the show was Peckham, South London,
and the show featured a predominantly Black British Guyanese cast
who in many cases caricatured the experiences of many West Indians
residing within the UK during this period. The programme provided
a relatable scene for many ethnic minority migrants, which positioned the barbershop as being a communal place of refuge from the

hostile environment encountered on a daily basis. Previous attempts at situating Black migrant life in the UK with a predominantly Black cast came in the form of *The Fosters*, adapted from the American sitcom *Good Times*, which ran for one year (April 1976–1977) featuring the two leaders of the Ambrose family, the late Norman Beaton who played Desmond Ambrose and Carmen Munroe who played Shirley Ambrose.

What resonated with most ethnic minorities during a time of high racial and political struggle nationally within the UK was the promise and aspiration to return to places of native birth, reconnecting spiritually and culturally; in the case of Desmond and Shirley Ambrose, this was Georgetown, Guyana, in the West Indies. The promise of social mobility, long before the arrival of New Labour was explored in *Desmond's* and repositioned Black people in an entirely different capacity from what the dominant discourse espoused. Desmond and Shirley were business owners during a racially and politically charged 1990s which at the time was unfathomable to a generation of ethnic minorities against a backdrop of institutional racism. Of their three children, Michael (Geff Francis) harboured ambitions to become a bank manager and endorsed a brand of capitalism that was not synonymous with Black people residing in the UK at the time; Gloria (Kimberly Walker) held aspirations of a job in the fashion industry; and Sean's (Justin Pickett's) main focus was to get into university. University still remains a substantive milestone for ethnic minorities, but during the 1990s access to the Academy was limited for people of colour wishing to become socially mobile through the vehicle of education (Modood and Acland, 1998). Such 'privileges' were reserved for the province of the White middle classes, with Blacks often having to gain access by navigating the landmine of institutional racism and inequality; such was the difficulty in attempting to access higher education at the time.

Desmond's helped to plant the seeds for multi-culturalism, integration, and diversity by building a narrative around culturally interchangeable characters that belonged to varying ethnicities including White, Asian, Chinese, and mixed heritage. In essence, this was really a thought-provoking representation of diversification and maybe an idealistic version of what Britain could be if navigated by the right type of inclusive politics. Although *Desmond's* provided culturally hilarious anecdotes, it also highlighted the existent prejudice, a visual conceptualisation many ethnic minorities could relate to internally and externally within their communities before and during the 1990s. Worrell adeptly portrayed the prejudice that existed not just between broad ethnic groups but also the within them, by centring the residual effects of colonial legacy. This was best contested in the comedy series between Desmond's childhood friend Porkpie, played by Ram John Holder, and eternal student Matthew, played by the late Gyearbour Asante, who became famed for pointing out the strength of African philosophical wisdom with what became his trademark regular interjection, 'there is an old African saying . . .'.

The point of reference for ethnic minorities was that they could see themselves reflected visually on television. Even as a socially aware child, the importance of this show was continuously reiterated to me as something that reflected the ethnic minority struggle. Although the death of Norman Beaton signalled the end of Channel Four's longest-serving sitcom, the show did leave a lasting impression that became an example to ethnic minorities of what could be aspirationally possible as an migrant within Britain, whether fictional or not. Meritocracy was still a fallacy, but the idea of social mobility for ethnic minorities was something that was becoming conceivable and *Desmond's* provided this narrative as a chorus for hope. It was also a stimulus for considering more impactful policy-driven interventions that needed to focus on better social and economic outcomes for Black people in Britain.

A reflection: disrupting racial stereotypes in the storm of Cool Britannia

Personally, my cognition of this dialogue was conflated within two particular instances within Black and White circles. As I began to dismantle racially stereotypical binaries within my own mind as a rock-loving, Vespa-riding, 60s Mod obsessive who harboured ambitions to dress like Paul Weller and strut like Oswald Boateng, I found myself marginalised from both Black and White social circles. White people were particularly precious and forthright about the type of individuals that should be granted membership into the 'Cool Britannia' brigade; unsurprisingly, a Black boy from Clapham, South London, did not quite fit the narrow, ignorant, racialised, and White prototype. Interestingly, the sense of marginalisation is not felt until I am reminded as a teenager that this is a 'British thing', not a Black thing, through some verbal but mostly symbolic acts of violence which reminds me of my presence as an ethnic minority and not as someone who had a verve for guitar music and sharp 60s Mod dressing. Negating this becomes difficult because the solace one anticipates receiving within their own ethnic community to some extent becomes nonexistent and this is shrouded in a narrative which conceptualises my indulgence of 'alternative music and fashion interests' as a betrayal of my Black heritage. Uniquely, and at several points during my teenage years, I found myself marginalised from both factions, which is interesting because this also repositions the narrative of cultural exclusion as perhaps something that is not exclusively White but rather societal. This often can be layered within several stereotypical binaries which assert that culturally it may be viewed as unacceptable to venture away from 'typical' conventions of stereotypical racial interest (Searle, 1973). At this point, an awareness ensues, in attempting to oscillate between 'cultures', that belonging is an innate concept which is often conceptualised through socialisation, acceptance, and cultural exposure.

The idea of love spreading throughout this period of time was entirely dependent on which social faction one belonged to. What became undeniable for me was three significant factors: first, that Britain is a racist country, always has been, and sadly always will be in some way, despite an eternally optimistic and idealist disposition; second, that there was an internal rejection of racial stereotypes or being labelled by White or Black people who may have had restrictive conceptions of how I should outwardly project or identify; and thirdly, that I had discovered myself and my political and social orientation that would navigate my moral compass for the rest of my adolescent, teenage, and adult life.

Conclusion

This chapter underlines the fact that the impact of the Cool Britannia years was not restricted only to those who were euphorically immersed within it. Ethnic minorities became a part of this discourse and understanding the racialised tensions of the time from both a personal and societal perspective help reshape the narrative and explore this phenomenon from a perspective of racial and cultural exclusion. The impact of New Labour regarding the racialised plight of multi-ethnic Britain was a timely and much-needed interjection which placed the issue of 'race and racism' on the political agenda. In doing so, it proffered an agenda that attempted to endorse cultural integration and better outcomes for Black and ethnic minority British residents. Attempting to understand a Britain that in some cases was reluctant to engage with the possibility of ethnic minority integration becomes the catalyst for further exploration into how multiple identities are constructed and accommodated through a restrictive and narrow paradigm of 'Britishness' that does little to embrace ethnic difference. Chapter 2 attempts to bring institutional racism into focus by exploring how this impacted Britain in the wake of the Stephen Lawrence murder, which subsequently led to the Macpherson Inquiry.

2   Don't look back in anger
Bringing institutional racism into public focus during the Cool Britannia years

Introduction

This chapter explores the canon of institutional racism and its subsequent impact on British society during the 1990s. The context for this, as mentioned earlier, is permeated by three events that would leave an indelible imprint on British societal history: the racially motivated murder of Stephen Lawrence, the induction of New Labour and its commitment to addressing inequality within British society, and the Macpherson Report. This chapter reflects in particular on the extent to which institutional racism permeated every facet of British society and the painstaking heroism of the Lawrence family in disrupting and detangling the cyclical web of racism that was sustained by the state and maintained through its major institutions.

Interspersed with retrospection and sadness, Oasis's 'Don't Look Back in Anger', from their second album release, *(What's the Story) Morning Glory* in 1995, has been deliberately appropriated in this treatise to capture the racial trauma that ensued at the time. The discourse of race and racism throughout the decade shifted between the sands of discrimination and deprivation, such was the extent and fluidity of the problem. The footnote provided by Oasis provides a metaphorical framework in attempting to understand the difficulties associated with reflecting upon a period in which the British state was culpable in facilitating an inequitable and discriminatory society through various institutional canons, resulting in further disadvantaging ethnic minorities in the process.

Articulating institutional racism in Britain

Although it is acknowledged that the first global articulation of the term institutional racism was initially coined by Stokely Carmichael (later known as Kwame Ture) and Charles V. Hamilton in *Black Power: The Politics of Liberation* (1967), it is universally accepted that the first enunciation of the term 'institutional racism' within a British context was proffered by the late, great Sri Lankan activist and novelist Ambalavaner Sivanandan. The scholar-activist is widely regarded as a bastion of the Race Relations movement and one of the leading Black political thinkers of our time within the UK. Sivanandan vehemently endorsed the liberation of Black people in the UK, often examining and illuminating the political economy of migration, decolonisation, and structured racism (Bourne, 2001; Hall, 1998). In his classic essay, 'Race, class and the state', he conceptualised institutional racism as being the problem of our time. Analysing the importance of the immigration acts from 1962–1971, Sivanandan declared that discrimination was out of the marketplace and given to the sanction of the state, thus making racism respectable and clinical by institutionalising it. Consequently, Sivanandan prophetically forecasted that this would increase the social and political consequences of racism. Institutionalised racism for Sivanandan was viewed as a construct which was inherent within the apparatuses of the state and the structures of an inequitable society, strategically embedded into the laws of the land, and then seamlessly interwoven into the judiciary and the executive (Gilroy, 1992; Yuval-Davis, 1999). Institutionalised racism described a systemic racism which became an instrument for facilitating power and privilege at the expense of Black and ethnic minorities (Bourne, 2001), an instrument of the state that has its legacy firmly rooted in supremacist structures and cultures that swept throughout inequitable Britain.

February 1999 would see a momentous and historical shift in equality reform, which sadly transpired from one of the most defining moments of the 1990s. Sir William Macpherson illuminated a long sequence of systemic racism which permeated all of society's major institutions in the wake of the Stephen Lawrence murder inquiry. Initially ordered by Jack Straw, Home Secretary from 1997 to 2001 under Blair, the most significant and consequential finding from the inquiry was the widespread landscape of institutional racism, particularly within MPS. Straw would subsequently state that his decision to order the inquiry would be 'the single most important decision that he made as Home Secretary'. Unsurprisingly, this verdict only confirmed to ethnic minorities what they had already known and experienced for a significant period of time through physical and symbolic racialised violence within Britain (Sivanandan, 1974). Previously forewarned by Sivanandan as 'the problem of our time', Macpherson (1999) declared that institutional racism played a significant part in the flawed and inexplicable corrupt investigation by the police in relation to the Lawrence murder. The historical legacy of racial inequality and discrimination led Macpherson to further assert that institutional racism was likely to be found in every organisation within the UK. For ethnic minorities already aware of this 'racism', there was now a tangible, working definition and a 'foothold for their discrimination' that encouraged societal institutions to examine their policies and the outcomes of their policies and practices in disrupting a legacy of racial disadvantage. Importantly, there was now a mandate for an unequivocal acceptance of institutional racism and its overt and covert characteristics which required immediate attention (Keith, 1993; Yuval-Davis, 1999; Macpherson, 1999). This was an undeniable watershed moment. Similarly, while Cool Britannia captivated a wave of nationalism, new politics, and optimism; the verdict of institutional racism gleaned the attention of policy-makers who could no longer deny the systemic and appalling landscape of racism that had swept throughout the UK. The toxicity of racism within a British context was laid bare for all to see and was visible even to those who indulged in the ignorant bliss of colour-blindness or post-racial Britain (Pilkington, 2003; Preston, 2010). Fundamentally, and perhaps idealistically, there was a collective consensus that this maybe was the agency needed for people of colour to truly flourish, become socially, politically, and economically mobile, in the hope that finally there was an appetite to embrace the potential for ethnic minority acceptance within British society (Neal, 2003; Shukra, 1998).

Although the concept of institutional racism was not a surprise to the ethnic minority population, perhaps Macpherson's verdict was, given that he was a privileged White, middle-class male with a somewhat disconnected understanding of racialised plights encountered in the UK before the commencement of the report (Sivanandan, 2006). Confidence in the process was further undermined because of the historical rarity in portraying absolute transparency and truth. Subsequently, when this verdict was returned in an alternative, racialised universe contrastingly different to that of the 'Cool Britannia utopia', this provided a 'cautionary' euphoria and optimism even for those severely scarred and battle-weary by decades of pernicious racism encountered as a Black and ethnic minority. Having such a concept thrust into the lexicon of national debate in the UK at the time, following the public inquiry into the failing of MPS regarding the racist murder of Stephen Lawrence, highlighted that those in the position to uphold Her Majesty's laws and objectives were in fact complicit in attempting to defame Lawrence, discredit his family, and absolve his murderers during the investigation (Hall, 1998; Yuval-Davis, 1999).

Such a watershed moment thrusted racism onto the political agenda, creating momentum for a renewed debate not just on the policing of minority communities but on the widespread discrimination within British institutions more generally. The eventual acceptance of the Inquiry's findings by the MPS Commissioner at the time, Sir Paul Condon, appeared to create a platform for catharsis and reconciliation with admissions of institutional racism from MPS, criminal justice agencies, and local government organisations (Singh, 2000; Souhami, 2007, 2014; Tonry, 2004). Initially, there was resistance from Condon, in which he obstinately refused to accept that his force was institutionally racist. What follows these admissions is profound, because for the first time the MPS as an institution found itself under acute and negative scrutiny and was finally made accountable for its deplorable actions, by both the media and by daily interactions with ethnic minority communities.

MPS now found itself quite ironically the subject of surveillance, under intense public and political pressure to urgently address the infestation of institutional racism that compromised its professionalism and made it complicit in initiating racism. Remembering that these were the custodians tasked with upholding Her Majesty's Laws and Objectives, for the first time, enforcers of the law were going to be held accountable. Rather belatedly, this systemic unveiling of racial discrimination would become a stimulus for protracted but nonetheless penetrative change (Warmington, 2009). The term 'institutional racism' became a legitimate vehicle which now had the weight of parliamentary influence behind it, something that can universally be credited to the Labour Government's attempted commitment to address racial disparity at the time regardless of party-political orientation. For ethnic minorities, this term provided a societal framework and facilitated an opportunity to conceptualise their racialised experiences within British society.

Recollections of the 1990s regarding this issue may differ for some, especially for those that were completely immersed within the Cool Britannia phenomenon. Even for those immersed within this cultural and historical episode, the conclusion passed by Macpherson forcibly drew everybody's attention and, perhaps for a generation of people, this was the first time that the stigmata of 'racism' became a collective issue that required a collective endeavour (Alleyne, 2002; Farrar, 2004). Historically, this most pernicious of issues had always been placed at the proverbial feet of those encountering the racial discrimination, rather than being tackled as a societal and national systemic problem. In particular, it is fair to say that the White middle-class had profited substantially from the terrain of inequity, so the onus was particularly on White middle-class males heading all of society's major institutions, first, to acknowledge their privilege and second, to relinquish some of that privilege in exchange for greater equity and access to particular types of economic, social, and cultural capital (Leonardo, 2005). The period, then as now, needed an intrinsic motivation on behalf of those afforded privilege which, in many cases, was unearned or inherited to dismantle the institutional racism. The onus was on the White middle class who had profited so handsomely from this inequity to diligently respond in supporting and advocating the need for greater diversification throughout society that was reflective of an ever-increasing multi-cultural Britain (Bourne, 2001; Solomos, 2003).

At the time, there was a feeling of change finally coming, perhaps signalling the beginning of a new mantra, aptly borrowed from Baddiel, Skinner & The Lightning Seeds's '*Three Lions*': 'it's coming home, it's coming home, it's coming . . . equality's coming home', as I recall someone gleefully singing to me. Sadly, such enthusiasm is always tempered with a hollowed chorus and caution; such is the omnipresent nature of racism and its ability to inflict continuous mental and physical lacerations on the beleaguered and battle-weary Black and ethnic minority community within Britain and globally.

The early to latter part of the 1990s was tinged with sadness for the inexplicable and needless loss of a promising young Black teenager. In a fleeting moment of pause and reflection towards the end of the 1990s, there was a consensus that it took a racially motivated, senseless murder at the hands of vile racists to bring the issue of epidemic racism into public consciousness (Hall, 1998; Woolley, 2011). The question which offers serious contemplation is: would the issue of 'institutional racism' even draw consideration had the late Stephen Lawrence not been brutally and senselessly slain? If the Lawrence's were the catalyst for challenging the state and all of its racially discriminatory procedures, then perhaps unfortunately and sadly, Stephen's murder provided the impetus for considering the much-needed widespread societal change.

As a teenager who bought into the notion of idealism that swept the nation at the time, there was a romanticism with the amalgamation of Cool Britannia and politics that sometimes removed me from my lived reality as a young Black male residing within a racist society. Innocence can sometimes be best articulated as representing idealisation and romanticism, with pragmatism reflecting an unfiltered reality which highlights that, without this seminal incident in our racialised history, it is likely that the issue of racism by the state would continue to remain ignored, unchallenged, and outside the margins of political discourse within mainstream British society (Hall, 1998; Alleyne, 2002; Bloch and Solomos, 2010). As an idealistic individual, this was an incredibly hard concept for me to digest, let alone grasp. At this point, there becomes a synergy with the racial discourse of the time which meant that rather than living in the Cool

Britannia utopia of today, an anti-racist consciousness needed to emerge which meant thought processes had to begin to think about the discriminatory and racialised landmine of tomorrow – a landmine which had already claimed a plethora of causalities, most notably a young, male, Black promising architect from South London.

A flawed history: attempting to conceptualise racism in Britain

The finding of institutional racism from a government-appointed judicial inquiry was a groundbreaking watershed moment for race relations within Britain. The working dialogue for racialisation was often referred to as the 'colour problem' by academics, the media, and social commentators (Tomlinson, 2008). As with most discriminatory discourse, the trivialisation of the problem was conceptualised as a psychological misunderstanding or clash of culture. However, the simplification of such an enduring epidemic demonstrates the marginal status that racism had occupied until the sanctioning of the Macpherson Inquiry in 1997.

Ethnic minority migrants during this time recognised some of the irrationality that accompanied racist rhetoric. In essence, this was interpreted as xenophobic activity; essentially, a natural fear of strangers (Gilroy, 1992, 2000). Interestingly, this is how Blacks were perceived in Britain . . . as strangers, space invaders, even after several decades of permanent residency as British citizens (Adi, 1995; Farrar, 2004). Through this lens, new Commonwealth immigrants represented the archetypal stranger by virtue of their skin colour. The prevailing narrative sought to present time and familiarity as the intermediary between prejudice and harmonious integration. However, the benefit of history is that it encapsulates a time period for us to explore, unpack, and examine. By the mid-1960s, Britain had already experienced its first 'race riots' (1958) and, perhaps cynically, politicians were on hand to convert this suffering to their advantage by exploiting racism and utilising this as an instrument to seduce voters, particularly in places such as Southall (West London) and in Smethwick (West Midlands), where the dialect of race becomes more complex and sophisticated (Sivanandan, 1974, 1982). Theories espoused all became conflated within government policies of 'immigration' and 'integration'. Immigration and integration reflected the potential for a contamination of all things fundamentally British and the national identity as a monolithically White state at the time (Adi, 1995; Banton, 1977; Gilroy, 1992).

For ethnic minorities in Britain, integration has always resembled assimilation, despite liberalist and idealist notions in theory of the term espoused by former Labour Home Secretary Roy Jenkins, who defined integration as 'equal opportunity accompanied by cultural diversity in an atmosphere of mutual tolerance' (Driver and Martell, 2006; Hindmoor, 2004). The history of racism in the UK and the reluctance to confront the issue until New Labour in 1997 suggests that this was never really prioritised as a pertinent political objective (Hall, 1998). The 1965 and 1968 Race Relations Acts outlawed 'overt' discrimination in a limited number of areas such as employment, housing, and the provision of goods and services, this context relied on conciliation rather than prosecution (Hall, 1998; HMSO, 1976; Gilroy, 1992). Acts such as these required a more expansive, intersectional reach if prejudice and discrimination within communities was to be reduced. Fundamentally, these acts did fall short in promoting a dialogue of inclusivity and multi-culturalism (Hall, 1990; Warmington, 2009). Its failure to directly tackle xenophobia in what was becoming a steadily increasing immigrant population was problematic (Warmington, 2009). Dominant narratives suggested a very constrained and narrow view of the plights that ethnic minority immigrants faced by simply suggesting that the problems faced were only cultural in nature (Farrar, 2004). The generalist approach suggested that they be allowed their own cultural 'space'. However, the effectiveness of this suggestion was solely dependent on White individuals at the time managing their personal prejudice, withholding abhorrent views of ethnic minorities, and embracing the idea of ethnic diversity (Neal, 2003; St. Louis, 2007). To embrace such difference and disrupt a firmly engrained notion of Britishness would invariably be problematic. This could be interpreted as the beginnings of stifling free speech, or the beginning of embracing multi-culturalism dependent upon which side of the fence one politically resides.

Other discourses provided the catalyst for challenging racism nationally. There was a sense of emancipation and empowerment within a burgeoning Black community, influenced by the uprising of Black Power politics and resistance within the US which resonated with the anti-colonial, oppressive struggle and lived racialised experience in the UK. However, the seeds of Black empowerment were metaphorically planted within a toxic soil, as the movement encountered a rear-guard action by nationalists who unashamedly voiced their disgust at being situated or housed next door to immigrant, non-White (British) neighbours (Bygott, 1992; Solomos, 2003; Owusu, 2000).

As previously mentioned throughout this treatise, this narrative was a reoccurring theme of the MPS's complicity in facilitating and peddling the racial, hostile environment. For Black people, the concerns that preoccupied thoughts, actions, and behaviours were centred around a causally racist public institution that was tasked with maintaining and enforcing the law (*Nigger Hunting in England* by Jo Hunte was published in 1965), a discriminatory educational system (Bernard Coard's *How the West Indian Child is Made Educationally Subnormal by the British School System* appeared in 1971), a biased and flawed criminal justice system (the 1971 Mangrove trial dismantled the myth of colour-blind justice), and immigration laws which not only divided families, but also cemented Black people's second-class status within the UK (Gilroy, 1992).

The clash of these two differing discourses has always been situated within policy-orientated interventions which have proved ineffective in alleviating the burden of racism for ethnic minorities. During the 1990s, there already had been an established consensus that race was not a political objective for the Conservative Party, which consequently resulted in a dearth of policy-driven interventions and research in this area that failed to build on the marginal gains of the 1965 Race Relations Act (Hall, 1990; Modood, 1992; Neal, 2003). During this period, there was an absence of penetrative, impactful policy-driven research that attempted to disrupt the centrality and monopoly of Whiteness within the UK as momentum was lost within the wake of the 1965 Race Relations Act with several government administrations at the helm, failing to address what had become an institutionalised problem that represented Britain as a nation that was not accepting of difference (Pilkington, 2003; Warmington, 2014). Sadly, this was heightened and encased within populism and fascism, disguised by the facade of nationalistic pride. The contextualisation of this discourse made it hard to situate 'Blackness' within Cool Britannia, as the context was not inclusive and, if anything, celebrated and heralded 'Britishness' as something that was White, not multi-cultural.

The hegemonic discourse in Britain on racism, described by Anthias and Yuval-Davis (1983, 1992) as Britain's 'Race Relations Industry', has tended for many years to be constructed towards a specific focus that has failed to encompass the whole range of racisms in Britain. As in other European cultures, the British heritage of racism (that is, of constructing categories of 'others' with immutable boundaries in order to exclude, make inferior, and exploit them) has included fascist and supremacist traditions of hatred towards Jews and Muslims as well as more broadly reported and conceived traditions of racism towards Black, Gypsy, and Traveller communities (Farrar, 2004; Marable, 1997). Racialised discourses developed mainly around notions of 'race' and 'colour' which were closely connected with Britain's historical past as an empire. Miles (1982) conceptualises this best by highlighting that the notion of 'race' as it emerged in the 19th century, served a dual purpose: to explain both hierarchy of interdependence between the English and colonial races, and the difference in productive relations and material wealth between England and much of the rest of the world at this time.

With the decline of the British Empire, the implementation of racialised discourses were systematically developed institutionally to reinforce White supremacy and establish discriminatory boundaries (Miles, 1989). Understanding this through the lens of what transpired through the 1990s is extremely pertinent when considering how ethnic minorities and migrants were excluded from celebrations of 'Britishness' (Alleyne, 2002). Paul Gilroy carefully points to the partiality clause in the British immigration law of 1968 as a common articulation of British nationalism and racism, codifying the 'cultural biology of "race" into statute law as part of a strategy for the exclusion of Black settlers' (Gilroy, 1992, p. 45). British race relations legislation, especially the 1965, 1968, and 1976 Acts, were passed specifically in order to combat racism (Yuval-Davis, 1999). However, there was a paradox inherent in these legislations: the Acts called for the elimination of various forms of racial discrimination while accepting the assumption that the population was indeed composed of people from different races (Banton, 1977; Gilroy, 1992). There was an inference that racism only affected predominantly Black individuals exclusively. The members of these races were identified in such laws as Section 11 of the 1966 Local Government Act as members of the New Commonwealth countries. Other forms of racism, directed at other racialised minorities, such as Gypsy Travellers, Irish, or Chinese, were mostly excluded from this discourse, as too were the racialised plights of the Jews and Arabs (Solomos, 2003).

The challenges to multi-culturalism and the growing rejection of the far-right from anti-racist activists and socialists in the 1990s brought about new directions which refined egalitarian perspectives from both political and theoretical paradigms. What ensued within the Cool Britannia years, particularly under New Labour ideology, was a rejection of essentialist notions of fixed culture and identity, which had typically characterised both multi-culturalism and anti-racism (Bhabha, 1994; Yuval-Davis, 1999). The re-evaluation of 'Britishness' under a New Labour Government provided the opportunity to reconceptualise culture and identity through a completely different lens, which attempted to endorse diversification as a vehicle for societal and cultural integration. Under the influence of post-structuralist and post-modernist theories, Yuval-Davis (1999) explains that culture became observed as being dynamic, syncretic, and a contested domain. Concepts such as diaspora (Brah, 1996; Bygott, 1992; Gilroy, 1992) became an instrument for challenging and centring the promise of multi-culturalism, in an attempt to overthrow the constrained and hostile typography regarding a re-imaging of the British landscape. This is beset by a changing narrative of Britishness that now has to acknowledge and accept the positive influence of Black labour, capital, and culture as a catalyst for advancing multi-culturalism in Britain:

> There is no longer a prevailing sense that what is British constitutes an ideal to which Black culture might want to aspire or assimilate. Thus, it is the very meaning and stability of Britishness itself which has been influenced by Black culture.
>
> (Hall, 1998, p. 40)

Feminist groups such as Women Against Fundamentalism (WAF) rejected the inherent assumption in multi-culturalism that all minority cultures are homogeneous and that the relationship of all members to their culture is the same (Sahgal and Yuval-Davis, 1992). This paints an important picture throughout the 1990s of how conflated the term 'multi-culturalism' became. Increasingly, it became harder for individuals and ethnic minorities to define this term as the dialect became fluidly interchangeable dependent upon the faction of society from which an individual derived. Above all, WAF challenged the notion that patriarchal community leaders should be given the authority to determine what constitutes 'authentic' culture and tradition regarding a specific community, arguing that the state was colluding in creating a space for the rise of new fundamentalist relationships (Gilroy, 1992). The interchanging dialogue and external interference from the state meant that the original charge of the anti-racist movement became derailed from its original mission of dismantling inequitable power relations between White and Black communities.

Conceptualised through this perspective, there is scope to suggest that cultural difference required a boarder canvas which required an acknowledgement of the wider context of citizenship rights and responsibilities. Importantly, considerations during this period needed to discern how existing governments could help transform Britain into a society that facilitated greater equity for all communities, ensuring equal access to housing and employment opportunities

(Banton, 1977; Solomos, 2003). There were previous indicators that the dominant discourse required re-examination, particularly when considering the racialised episodes that set the precedent for a misunderstanding of cultural difference and acceptance from within British society. The Brixton riots that preceded the factious 1990s and the subsequent Scarman Report (1981) which arose from these events characterised approaches towards fighting racism. Although there was an increased focus on representation and ethnic monitoring as a result of the riots, the term 'Black' became a category which replaced such terms as 'West Indians' or 'Afro-Caribbeans'. This submersion was extended to Asians, who generally were categorized as 'Black' typically politically. To this end, the term 'Asian' remained in ethnic monitoring vernacular to signify and differentiate individuals from the Indian subcontinent (Anthias and Yuval-Davis, 1992; Modood, 1992; Solomos and Back, 1996). The 1990s redefined these terms because of the renewed emphasis on culture, which saw the growing politicisation and demonisation of Muslims and Islam as an instrument for radicalisation and terrorism, consequently making it even harder for migrant workers and refugees to assimilate as ethnic and cultural minorities. This presents another example of how racism reinvented itself within the political and societal context at the time, giving rise to the articulation of new anti-racist terms such as 'cultural racism' (Banton, 1977; Modood, 1992).

Understanding racialised boundaries within British society

During a time of high political struggle, the 1990s did raise a generational awareness of racialised campaigns, most notably from the inspirational plight of Winnie and Nelson Mandela's rise to prominence as the mother and father of a New South Africa to the success of the Stephen Lawrence campaign, which brought much-needed focus to anti-racist campaigns nationally and globally. The emergent rejection of racial inequality provided a catalyst which sought to dismantle racism and the power and privilege that accompanies this as the normative orthodoxy. The emergent theme which arose from

the murder of Stephen Lawrence illuminated how the police con-
spired to handle this particular case. Subsequently, this transcended
perceptions about the effectiveness of anti-racism movements and
campaigns. The pressure exerted by the Lawrences and the imped-
ing change of government at the time played a major part in understanding how major British societal institutions had been complicit
in historically and judicially failing ethnic minorities, consequently
perverting several cases of justice whilst perpetuating racial inequality and discrimination (Yuval-Davis, 1999). This was best exemplified in the attempt to assassinate Lawrence's character and racially
ascribe him as a proponent of criminality. It also exposed the Conservatives as a party that had entirely no interest in tackling racial
discrimination and improving race relations within Britain. We can
therefore safely assert that the Macpherson Report and subsequent
race relations interventions that followed would not have come to
fruition under Tory governance.

The anti-racism campaigns of the 1990s facilitated a tectonic shift
in anti-discriminatory discourse which endorsed new ways of viewing British national connectedness. However, the continual criminalisation of Black males did create a hesitance in the gradual acceptance
of Black and ethnic minority individuals into British society (Gilroy,
1987; Solomos and Back, 1996). Unfortunately, during the 1990s
and beyond, this continued to be an enduring 'hallmark' of racial
profiling and ascription. Contrastingly, the criminalisation of White
'football hooligans', many of whom had been closely affiliated with
the Extreme Right, were celebrated as nationalists defending Britannia. Comparatively, the continued characterisation of young Black
males as 'criminals' became desensitised to divisions of class, in
essence 'Blackness' became a symbol of criminality (Hall, 1998).
During the time, stories typically involved and reported Black males
as being routinely stopped and searched without basis, reason, or
foundation. The Home Office was notorious for being typically slow
to respond or prioritise this as a matter of national or state urgency.
This indecisiveness to act garnered a public response of indignation
concerning the way Stephen Lawrence and his family were treated
by the police, as they attempted to proffer an anti-racist discourse

that was contradictory to their discriminatory and confrontational engagement with ethnic minorities. The wrongful attempt to portray and perpetuate a negative and criminalised stereotype of what became the atypical Black man within British society was distinguished at every possible juncture by the Lawrence family. There was a determination to dismantle the dominant discourse and provide a discourse that disrupted such an ignorant and racialised supremacist notion (Mirza, 1997; Solomos, 2003).

On the contrary, the Lawrences, Stephen in particular, represented a well-educated young Black man from a middle-class family. Conversely, but not any less importantly, how may have this been portrayed in the public domain if this was an individual excluded from school with a fractured family unit? It is safe to assert that the police may have been even less objectionable in their attempts to exploit such a narrative. However, this did represent (similar to the *Desmond's* narrative) that the Lawrences were on the 'right' side of the class spectrum, representing to varying degrees particular types of social, cultural, and economic capital associated with being upwardly socially mobile. At this point, there were modest indications that suggested ethnic minorities were beginning to become recognised and accepted as a legitimate part of the British landscape with all the capabilities to be socially mobile, most notably under a New Labour Government endorsing greater economic mobility for all members of society (Hindmoor, 2004).

The mid-1990s revealed an emerging and public resistance towards crude and racialised behaviours which were no longer justifiable by large sections of the British population (Yuval-Davis, 1999). The national dialogue was changing. Ethnic minority points of reference were becoming more visible throughout British society and this would significantly contribute to shifting the negative and distorted paradigm that beset people of colour within the UK. Trevor McDonald had cemented his iconic status as the nation's leading newsreader in the UK, having first graced our screens in 1973. He would be knighted in 1999 for services to broadcasting and journalism and was dubbed by *The Independent* as 'the voice of middle England'. This adulation extended beyond the newsroom into the

sporting arena. The British public at the time extended their acceptance of ethnic minorities by extoling elevated status to former boxing two-weight world champion Nigel Benn and the incomparable
former world middleweight champion Christopher Livingstone
Eubank, who became a fantastic dance partner for Benn and one of
the longest-reigning British world boxing champions. This status
would also be famously extended to the 2000 Sydney Olympics and
Double Commonwealth Heptathlon champion Denise Lewis, who
would help to redefine the dominant and often negative discourse
concerning not only ethnic minorities but Black women in particular. These examples of 'successful' Black Britons would go on to
be enshrined in British folklore. Their presence would subsequently
punctuate the minds of the British public in terms of the way ethnic
minorities had historically been portrayed negatively by the British
press. There is an acceptance that this may be speculative in conjecture but the partial example of prominent Black figures within British
popular subculture and society could have been a potential reason for
the swell of support for the Stephen Lawrence inquiry in virtually all
of the popular press, and in particular the *Daily Mail*, which in February 1997 took the unprecedented step of naming the five suspects
involved in Stephen's murder, who had, in a cowardly move, pleaded
for anonymity (Yuval-Davis, 1999).

Generally speaking, since that particular incident the media industry has shown modest advances in attempting to be more objective
in the reporting of racist incidents. However, it is also fair to suggest
that these modest advances have been eclipsed by continuous negative character assassinations of ethnic minorities within the UK and
racial profiling (Mirza, 1997; Warmington, 2013). The need to provide news coverage that was sympathetic to the plight of racism and
fascism that percolated throughout Britain was gaining momentum.
There was a caution that ensued, mindful of indulging a new optimism or being misled into thinking that upon this basis Britain had
somehow become a less-racist and more-tolerant society. The potential indulgence of this particular panacea failed to acknowledge the
doggedness and stubbornness of racism as a decisive and persistent

instrument that was and remains continually able to invent itself through other insidious and covert forms (Alexander, 1996; Alleyne, 2007). The continuous reinvention of racism sustained by the British media has been influential in spinning a dominant and often negative discourse regarding Black people and ethnic minority migrants.

Interestingly, the hegemonic discourse on racism in Britain which emerged as Britain's 'Race Relations Industry' during the 1990's often failed to encompass the entire spectrum of racisms in Britain. Through this lens it became paramount to view citizenship and diversification as a multi-layered construct, in which one's citizenship is viewed through varying levels of connectivity that encompass local, ethnic, national, and the state. This working definition was problematic because of a failure to acknowledge how relational and positional factors impact specific historical contexts concerning the integration of ethnic minorities (Adi, 1995; Kundnani, 2007). The events of the time led to a revaluation of approaches by the police, state, and other civil society agencies which required prominent stakeholders to value 'cultural diversity' and acknowledge the differential power relations within inter- and intra-communal factions. As a consequence, New Labour's intention became a lot more focused on evolving the dialogue of the anti-discriminatory discourse from not only identity and acceptance of difference but also to greater equality outcomes for an ever-increasing ethnic minority migrant population during the 1990s (Driver and Martell, 2006; Preston, 2010).

Notions of difference that encompass the broad church of equality are not hierarchical and require a respect for varying intersectional nuances and complexities, particularly where cultural integration is concerned. Such considerations of differential social, economic, and political power provide a framework for conceptualising the idea of belonging and citizenship within a British context. Conceptualising through this lens provided the basis for a new brand of dialogical, transversal citizenship which attempted to liberate the 1990s of the historical, racialised, and constrained view of ethnic minority migration (Anthias and Yuval-Davis, 1992; Bloch and Solomos, 2010; Yuval-Davis, 1994). The notion of multi-layered transversal citizenship in which difference encompasses equality outlines the difficulties faced during the 1990s and presently in how this concept could be successfully achieved. At the time of dissemination, it was particularly hard to decipher how impactful the Macpherson Report would be in providing the institutional catalyst needed to ignite wide-sweeping reform of policy-driven measures and governmental change towards reframing citizenship (Pilkington, 2013; Yuval-Davis, 1999). Nearly two decades on, there has been a steady diversification of our major institutions within society which has attempted to endorse multi-cultural agency as a way to modernise and create a more integrative Britain. The caveat to this, unfortunately, is that we still reside in a Britain where pockets of inhabitants strongly reject evolving definitions of citizenship, migration, and integration (Modood, 2007; Parekh, 2006). This became exacerbated as the chasm between the rich and poor grew larger, particularly for ethnic minorities struggling to gain access to opportunities to become socially and economically mobile within an institutionally racist context (Parekh, 2006).

Defining and implementing a working definition of institutional racism

At the time and maybe even presently, there still sometimes remains some confusion about how we politically and correctly define institutional racism. Some of the blame for this confusion between structural and personal racism has to be laid at Macpherson's door because it was his articulation of institutional racism, in attempting to be exhaustive, that inadvertently ended up causing ambiguity. In the hands of the far-right, the perceived lack of clarity regarding the definition was ammunition for exploitation. The inquiry utilised a definition of the concept which articulated institutional racism as:

> The collective failure of an organisation to provide an appropriate and professional service to people because of their colour, culture or ethnic origin. It can be seen or detected in processes, attitudes and behaviour which amount to discrimination through

unwitting prejudice, ignorance, thoughtlessness and racist stereotyping which disadvantage minority ethnic people.

(Macpherson, 1999)

Although Macpherson correctly identified organisations' collective
failure – most notably their aggregate failure and failure as a whole –
as the crux of the problem, there was an oversight in locating such
failure in societal structures, workings, and the culture of organisations, which includes not only processes, behaviour, policies,
practices, and procedures, but also the organic relationship between
them and the discriminatory dynamics that emerge as a result (Gilroy, 2000; Modood, 2007; Lammy, 2011). Perhaps rather naïvely
and simplistically, Macpherson attributed this collective failure in
part to individual attitudes and behaviour. By individualising this,
Macpherson inadvertently absolved British society as a structure
that facilitated racism. The absence of a need for collective respon-
sibility within British society for racism as a divisive and discriminatory instrument conflicted with anti-racist resistance movements
attempting to dismantle the inequitable structure (the state) that
upholds racism (Bourne, 2001). Proclamations such as 'unwitting
prejudice' and 'thoughtlessness' further compounded the confusion
between personal and institutional racism, providing leverage for
further resistance to the term by those with no appetite for racial
equity or eliminating racism entirely (Bloch and Solomos, 2010;
Bourne, 2001).

Despite the prevailing ambiguities in his definition, Macpherson
did emphasise within his government recommendations regarding the
MPS that the force as an institution was racist, adding that outcome
rather than (racial) motivation was central to racially discriminatory
occurrences (Macpherson, 1999). Primarily, this was the reason for
passing a recommendation that the 'full force' of the 1976 Race Relations Act be brought to bear on the any form of law enforcement.
The term 'full force' implied that special provisions were required
in ensuring that the police would no longer be complicit in indirect
or direct racial discrimination. Macpherson's proclamation recognised the introduction of indirect discrimination in 1976 to cover and

apprehend discrimination that occurs 'irrespective of motive' (Hall, 1998; Yuval-Davis, 1999). This remains significant because, up until that point, all government and institutional bodies historically had been exempted from the provisions of the Race Relations Act (Hall, 1998).

The Lawrences: a lasting legacy

Although the Macpherson Report remains a continual work in progress, the unlikely emergence of a humble, reserved, and stoic heroine from the tragedy of the Stephen Lawrence murder, who became a symbol for forgiveness, restraint, and dignity, remains the lasting legacy from this inquiry. Baroness Doreen Lawrence occupies a very special place in the lexicon of the British political and judicial system and in society more generally. Her enforced involvement in British politics has facilitated greater measures of equity and legal rights for ethnic minorities within the criminal and judicial system throughout the UK. Her influence was such that on the day the Macpherson Report was published, Tony Blair publicly asked for her assistance in helping to eradicate racism from British society – such was the gravitas of her influence. The Lawrences' demand for justice represented a mandate for equality for the entire Black populace, who had been systematically victimised and oppressed throughout British societal history. The perseverance of the Lawrences came to represent and symbolise the demand for justice for all those that had been racialised and marginalised at the hands of the institutionally racist British justice system. The tenacity, persistence, and intelligence of the grief-stricken parents represented a reframing of politics that symbolised the divisive effect of racism within our society, particularly when not addressed or dealt with politically and publicly.

The dignified and unwantedly forced interjection of the Lawrences at a time of racially and politically charged tension within society during the 1990s has now become an enduring symbol for the democratisation of British society. Unsurprising and consequently, this family have become a beacon for equality and equity for the ethnic minority populace within the UK. Their enduring legacy has been their successful attempt to redefine 'Britishness' as a concept that needed to institutionally address all of its discriminatory and oppressive regimes which had for so long disadvantaged, dehumanised, and marginalised ethnic minorities.

A reflection: learning the language of racism

Learning the language of racism and discrimination is in many ways enforced and experiential. Definitions of the term can, through varying levels of ignorance, become conflated within many contexts. Understanding how racism impacts ethnic minorities can be very distressing to observe because these experiences occur through a myriad of racialised instruments. There has always been an idealistic contemplation which queried, what if racism did not exist? Would another oppressive structure occupy its place? History tells us that within a society in which there is uncontested patriarchy, the emotional and physical labour of a minority group will always be exploited, normally involving some form of oppression, inequality, enslavement, or discrimination. Sadly, there is a high probability that some form of oppression may exist in its place. Racism is an interesting precursor to a lot of daily experiences encountered by ethnic minorities in particular. For the entirety of my childhood and adolescence, through the news, media, and other social commentaries, there were permanent reminders of how this form of subordination works within society. In truth, my parent's racialised experiences as migrants within the UK prepared me for what to potentially expect for the rest of my life as a British domiciled citizen. However, no amount of forewarning prepares an individual for the first time they encounter a discriminatory episode which dehumanises and renders them inadequate or less-than. Such a discriminatory experience can be life-defining. When these experiences become routinely part of one's daily existence in the world of work, education, or wider society generally, then this becomes a war of attrition. People of colour can be credited with many things throughout the course of history in the face of overwhelming victimisation, dehumanizstion, brutality, oppression, and discrimination, but perhaps their most enduring quality is their ability to be continually and eternally resilient (Hall, 1998). Encountering and negotiating racism on a continual basis requires a dignity and restraint that is unimaginable for someone who has not had to evade the toxic and racialised discriminatory swamp. To the individual permanently on the margins of equality, this is a reality that those fortunate to reside within the margins may find hard to understand, conceptualise, or comprehend. Traversing this terrain involves a continuous fighting of the tide which can subsume ethnic minorities and contribute to difficulties in obtaining access to opportunities to become socially mobile and economically self-sufficient (Hall, 1990).

As a younger person aware of the perils of racism, you are presented with a handful of opportunities in comparison to your White counterparts, and to this end constant parental reminders were proffered, stating that no matter what you do, you will always have to work harder than a White person to get an opportunity or get ahead. Perhaps what was not anticipated was the lifelong burden and residual effects of continually encountering racism, which in truth exhaust mentally and physically, taking a toll on psychological faculties.

Effectively, Macpherson's report attempted to address the unfairness of this unrequested lifelong burden for ethnic minorities against a backdrop of racial discrimination and inequality, consequently confirming Sivanandan's previous proclamation that Britain as a society was intuitionally racist. Sivanandan was right to assert that this would be 'the problem of our time', such is the centrality and permanency of racism. Though it has undertaken various reincarnations, the roots of racism are firmly engrained within the fabric of British tapestry. As a young teenager at the time, cognisant of the fraught and racially tense political and societal climate, I felt that the Macpherson Report highlighted to me that if one attempts to view this judgement with a mind unclouded by ideological sophistry or political gain, then it is impossible to ignore that our major institutional organisations are contaminated by structures, cultures, and procedures which inherently reproduce and sustain racism (Bourne, 2001).

Our institutional racist structures very much facilitate the skewed notion that prejudice is something that, if kept to oneself, was of no great concern. Verbalising an inequitable experience resides within a backdrop of 'what's a little racism . . . Blacks should be just grateful to be here, they are too hyper-sensitive'. Strangely, the reporting of racism was often considered to institutionally disrupt a 'harmonious' British society. The feeling that often preceded racist reporting positioned ethnic minorities as wanting to create racial fiction between Blacks and Whites. Such a rhetoric often further compounded the wounds inflicted by overt and covert racism. The thought processes that accompany prejudice can be unknowing or unconscious when adopting the solace or safer ground of residing within a post-racial or colour-blind society (Bell, 1992).

It is not merely the acting out of (individual) prejudice that makes for (social) discrimination, it is the tacit, prejudiced thoughts that accompany this which can potentially become discriminatory actions. Thus, when such discrimination becomes ingrained in the psyche of individuals and institutions of society, it becomes institutional racism. There was a clear oversight from Macpherson which overlooked the symbiosis between institutional racism and state racism. In fact, state racism is completely overlooked altogether. This glaring omission failed to recognise that from a societal perspective it is in fact the state – the legislature, the executive, the judiciary, through its immigration and asylum laws, its administration of public services (such as the police, prisons, immigration), and its courts and Crown Prosecution Service – that sets the tone and tenor for race relations within society (Bourne, 2001). Although a much-needed framework was provided for conceptualising and outlawing institutional racism in public bodies, there appeared to be a contradiction which still facilitated racist immigration and asylum laws and restrictions on jury trials and prohibited specific refugee organisations within legislation – all of which subsequently affected Black people and refugees in particular (Hiro, 1972; Bourne, 2001).

Racism is not episodic; it is a continuous stream of discrimination that has historically perched on the shoulders of inequality and inequity. The fight against institutional racism, therefore, cannot only be seen through a singular anti-racist paradigm, it requires several approaches to dismantle the larger shadow of state racism which maintains asylum laws and deportation laws and endorses stop and search as an instrument to habitually incarcerate young Black men. State racism also facilitates ethnic minority deaths in custody and the school exclusions of young Black pupils, and enables miscarriages of justice. Thus, attempts to combat popular racism cannot be undertaken without combating the state racism which provides popular racism with its impetus (Bourne, 2001). Simply put, state racism severely sullies and contaminates civil society; when you consider how Black and ethnic minorities reflect on this intense period, it is understandably quite hard not to look back in anger.

Conclusion

Debates over the impact of institutional racism have continued to perplex, even in the wake of the Macpherson Report. This chapter attempted to present an overview of how racism has been historically weaponised by the state to marginalise, oppress, and dehumanise Black and ethnic minority individuals within Britain. The chapter explored the complicity of MPS in the unlawful miscarriage of justice regarding the murder of Stephen Lawrence, which would subsequently highlight the perniciousness of racialisation and the centrality it occupied within all of societies major institutions.

The legacy of trivialisation regarding racism within Britain became a focal point in this chapter that helps to unpack how 'multiculturalism' was engaged with throughout the 1990s and the idea that this concept would threaten to distil imperialistic notions of Britishness. Interestingly, for all its myriad of racialised, communal, and contextual problems, as Warmington asserts, multi-culturalism helped to shape political blackness and the activism that propels this resistance. The legacy of the Lawrence family in this regard allows us to continually redefine this term politically in accommodating the ever-changing and diverse context that is multi-ethnic Britain. In the final chapter of this book, the provided contexts attempt to summarise the Cool Britannia period, specifically highlighting the impact of this phenomenon on ethnic minorities by exploring and unpacking anti-racist resistance movements during the 1990s and the inevitable rejection from the far-right for greater racial equality.

3 Bittersweet symphony
Reflecting and drawing conclusions on the Cool Britannia years in multi-ethnic Britain

Introduction

This book began by discussing and unpacking the subcultural whirl-wind that was Cool Britannia. The influence that the period had in marginalising ethnic minorities by culturally excluding them ensured that they remained on the periphery of this phenomenon. Contexts explored also acknowledge the impact of New Labour on challenging institutional racism in the wake of the Macpherson Report and their attempt to bring racial discrimination from the political margins to the centre. This chapter further reflects on this period by exploring the impact of anti-racist movements and drawing conclusions on how racism transpired as the decade progressed. Considerations throughout the chapter will also consider discourses that emerged, particularly around cultural integration and the inevitable rejection for racial equality by the far-right in Britain at the time.

Summarising the 1990s can be quite difficult, because it was one of the most definitive decades of the 19th century. This was an era defined by music, sub-culture, politics, and racism. But perhaps, no other song captures the compelling narrative of the time better than The Verve's anthemic Bitter Sweet Symphony in 1997, from the band's third studio album *Urban Hymns*, a track that subtly and poignantly presents the oxymoron of life by capturing the euphoria and depression one can encounter simultaneously while traversing the everyday rigours of life. This particular song becomes a metaphoric point of departure in considering some of the complexities of racism, from celebrating the marginal gains of the Macpherson Report to the resurgence of the far-right. This track in many ways provides a soundtrack to the continuous racism that reverberated within Britain and the lack of recognition by the state in attempting to alleviate the burden of social and racial inequality for ethnic minorities at the time, despite the recommendations provided by Macpherson.

Mobilising multi-ethnic Britain: what was the New Labour legacy regarding race equality?

Although this can be contested, the dawn of New Labour was instrumental for ethnic minority communities in Britain. The most common charge made against Blairism was that it represented an inevitably unsuccessful attempt to please all of the people all of the time (Driver and Martell, 2006; Heffernan et al., 2016). There was a point at which New Labour needed to assess the extent of its true commitment to radical change. The lack of clarification regarding this commitment became a criticism that gathered force as New Labour became eager to win a second term in government, while struggling to reassure the more prosperous and conservative of its belief in market forces and family stability (Hindmoor, 2004; Parekh, 2000). Perhaps the juxtaposition that emerged presented Blair's Labour as a government that sought to reach for the moral high ground of radical change while continuing perpetual 'modernity' in politics (Bourne, 2001). This was best conceptualised by Baroness Doreen Lawrence, who queried the government's record on race when demanding a reform of the police service, stating: 'they want to implement changes but they want to please middle England as well'. This assertion was indeed powerful and accurate, as New Labour unsuccessfully attempted to satisfy an increasingly split and disenfranchised Britain (Hindmoor, 2004). It was on the fundamental issue of poverty and social justice that New Labour's policies were routinely juxtaposed against other intersectional metrics such as disability, class, religion, and gender (Bourne, 2001).

On reflection, however, one could assert from a subjective disposition that here was a government passionate about the provision of opportunity for all its citizens – a chorus that resonated with ethnic minority communities in Britain, who had long been peripheral in regards to access and opportunity on these shores (Preston, 2010). New Labour's commitment to social justice was reflected during the tail end of the 1990s, with the introduction of an impressive array of anti-poverty measures, including the New Deal in employment, a comprehensive strategy for neighbourhood and community renewal, Health and Education Zones, the Sure Start programme to support deprived babies and young children, the National Child Care Strategy, tax credits, and the national minimum wage (Driver and Martell, 2006; Hindmoor, 2004). This also was the first government ever to create a unit specifically dedicated to tackling the problem of 'social exclusion'. The establishment of SEU in December 1997 produced several reports focused on truancy and school exclusion; rough sleeping; teenage pregnancy; 16- and 18-year-olds who were not in education, jobs, or training; the accessibility of information technology; and neighbourhood renewal (Driver and Martell, 2006; Heffernan et al., 2016).

To many within the Labour Party at the time, SEU was the jewel in Labour's policy crown, its favoured administrative centrepiece. The introduction of these positive social inclusion interventions was much needed. However, within the embattled trenches of Black and anti-racist politics, there was great anticipation and an expectancy that change was beginning to gather some sustained momentum. There were criticisms suggesting that Labour took a similar disposition to the Conservatives on race, pandering to the gallery and delivering very little beyond the Macpherson Report, which arguably highlighted something most ethnic minorities already knew (Sivanandan, 2006). In comparison to Labour, it is safe to assert that the Conservatives have a questionable record on issues concerning race equality and dealing with racism generally in Britain.

The commitment to modernising Britain was extremely important; it signalled the potential for something ethnic minorities had not experienced and continue not to experience in all its virtues: equality. Yet, there was a sense that the Labour Government at the time did at least attempt to embrace the idea of cultural diversity and equality by placing institutional racism on to the political agenda (Solomos, 2003). Indeed, the proliferation of diversity discourse coincided with the civil unrest regarding the steady acceptance of multi-culturalism. The drive towards a more inclusive society was clearly extended to issues of race, which consumed a significant part of the 1990s. At times during this period there was a problematic celebration of cultural diversity which placed significant pressure on Blair's Labour Government to uphold their commitment to addressing some of the more pernicious long-standing forms of racial discrimination (Bourne, 2001). More than two decades have passed since the installation of Blair's New Labour Government and since that period we have somewhat observed a different emphasis in polices, maybe even a regression regarding the preservation of ethnic minority rights and liberties, most notably through urban regeneration initiatives and the resounding call for a tightening of borders to reduce migrant intake within Britain (Bourne, 2001; Solomos, 2003). Policy changes during the 1990s and beyond continue to raise a series of questions ranging from racial inequality to wider aspects of social exclusion. Indeed, policies pursued by governments since 1997 have focused on a combination of localised, short-term initiatives to deal with deprivation within communities aimed at addressing and rebalancing aspects of social exclusion and marginalisation (Mirza, 1997). The Labour manifesto at the time attempted to focus on developing an urban policy that focused on regenerating some of the UK's most deprived and decaying areas that had been neglected in the wake of the Thatcher years (Bourne, 2001).

The decade itself was punctuated by a staunch resistance to anti-racist policies at local and national levels, but despite these populist protestations race and ethnicity would finally become an established part of the political landscape at the time which meant that in the face of growing globalisation and increased diversification within Britain, changes had to be made to better safeguard ethnic minorities and migrant workers (Kundnani, 2007). It is undeniable that race continues to remain a perennial feature at the frontbench of national politics because of its enduring nature in facilitating discrimination and inequality. There still are issues that permeate access to opportunity, education, and employment for ethnic minorities (Lammy, 2011). However, what New Labour achieved towards the tail end of the 1990s, going into the new millennium, was a sense of hope that endorsed the potential for all members of society to be socially mobile, particularly those from ethnic minority groups who had endured continuous discrimination and inequality that at times seemed unrelenting, sustained, and hostile (Bourne, 2001; Owusu, 2000). Understanding this from the point of optimism is significant because there was a time when race relations seemed at breaking point and unrepairable, particularly after the Stephen Lawrence murder. The 1990s were, if nothing else, very durable and resilient, often surmounting and hurdling one racially charged fence after another. As an adolescent, I had an awareness that, against these problems, there was always the all-encompassing backdrop of Cool Britannia that attempted to subsume varying narratives in attempting to portray an inclusive and cohesive Britain that was not racially discriminatory in any way.

Operating on the periphery of the Cool Britannia years

The media play a crucial role in informing society about everyday issues; perhaps unsurprisingly, their stance on race during the 1990s was pretty nuanced and partisan, despite the increasing global attention on the racialised plights of America, South Africa, and Great Britain. Media interest was funnelled through British youth culture magazines which were actually not reflective of the ethnic minority population at the time. Many of the British magazines were heavily situated within a dominant White narrative. This was encapsulated by two particular fashion magazines, *The Face* and *Loaded*, and, two music magazines, *New Musical Express* and *Q*. These were the most definitive magazines of the time and were considered generally to be the most representative of British youth culture in the 1990s. Perhaps unsurprisingly, this was not representative of ethnic minorities. Often, this provided a platform to herald and celebrate predominantly the success of White Britons within the arts and subculture, completely omitting the cultural influence and impact of people of colour (Alleyne, 2007). Such processes of exclusion further exacerbated feelings of residing on the margins of this definitive period in British history. Although ethnic minorities were omitted from this dominant discourse, their presence could not be ignored, due to the increasing number of high-profile cases which illuminated the reality of racial violence within the UK. The murder of Stephen Lawrence gleaned the most attention; however, there were other significant cases such as Quddas Ali, Micheal Menson, Ricky Weel, and Mukhtar Ahmed (Lammy, 2011; Solomos, 2003). These particular cases became lost within the Cool Britannia vortex. A report undertaken by Human Rights Watch in 1997 highlighted the extent of racial violence in Britain and the relative weakness in legislation addressing this issue and dismantling structures of racism (Yuval-Davis, 1999).

The mobilisation of race is continually evolving and this makes it difficult to stay abreast of this particular unrelenting curve. Throughout and beyond the 1990s this has been demonstrated by the emergence of new forms of racist politics and violent attacks on ethnic minority and migrant populations, further adding to the cyclical impact of a state that facilitates structural racism. Although the 1990s were punctuated by a rapid expansion of neo-fascist movements towards the end of the decade, a gradual shift in perception began within British society. Society was becoming more cognisant of the racialised plights experienced by Black communities, through considerable journalistic attention (an obvious consequence of the Macpherson Report) highlighting the impact of ever-increasing racist activities and their impact on particular factions of British society (Woolley, 2011). Political stalwarts such as Baroness Valarie Amos, Baroness Sayeeda Warsi, and Diane Abbott MP rallied on the frontline in an attempt to glean more awareness within the political arena and wider community on the issue of racism and its debilitating effects for ethnic minority communities in Britain.

The climax of the 1990s would demonstrate a strengthening and political mobilisation of far-right movements across Britain and Europe, carefully choreographed through international networks which were successfully able to reinforce their own virulent, nationalistic patterns of racism (St. Louis, 2007). The growth and mobilisation of the internet during the 1990s facilitated broader modes of communication that transcended national boundaries ensuring a global and electronic platform for race hatred. The growth of racism during this period, whether directed at new targets or expressed through varying media platforms, observed a resurgence of traditional racist movements which were couched within a nationalist or populist rhetoric. Aspects of this xenophobia would invariably be conflated within much of the Cool Britannia phenomenon as endorsing a sense of national pride in all things specifically British and, by proxy, White. There was an inevitable derailing and disruption of anti-racist movements as complacency began to occupy the space of proactivity regarding the fight for racial equality. There was a fear among anti-racists that, despite having a Labour Government that attempted to prioritise race equality, faction of Britain were continuing to espouse and purport dominant racist ideologies which would create hostile environments for ethnic minorities (Adi, 1995; Alleyne, 2007; Gilroy, 2000). This would inevitably consume the political agenda, which compromised any forward momentum and positive gains from the Macpherson Report regarding developing and improving race relations within Britain.

Racist stereotyping became a more impactful soundtrack during the 1990s and beyond. This racism extended to refugees and economic migrants, through a discriminatory and fascist discourse which typically placed emphasis on negative social and cultural characteristics (Alleyne, 2007; Mirza, 1997). When considered through differing national contexts, it has historically been safe to assert that this will differ from one context to another. The culture and fluidity of the extreme right during the 1990s posed real difficulties regarding specifically defining their racist activity. In many ways, the extreme right proved to be rather elusive as a movement, often targeting ethnic minority groups in secluded and isolated circumstances in large predatory groups, with the liberty of being able to masquerade and drift between multiple identities, from football hooligan to chief executive officer (Solomos and Back, 1996), utilising varying tools of Whiteness to enact their brand of unfiltered racism. A wide range of terms, including neo-Nazi, White supremacist, fascist, and racist, were used to describe the wide range of ideologies, movements, and groups (Solomos and Back, 1996). Interestingly, there was a set of characteristics and features that defined these particular factions:

- A rhetoric of racial and/or national uniqueness and common destiny;
- The idea of racial supremacy and superiority;
- A conception of racial otherness;
- A utopian revolutionary worldview that promotes the overthrow of the existing order.

(Solomos, 2003, p. 184)

The context provided speaks to the influence of particular societal canons such as politics, culture and the mass media. A distinctive feature that becomes apparent in unpacking belongingness and otherness is the continual enforced reinvention of ethnic minorities to adapt to an ever-changing and racialised vernacular of belonging within a British context. Historically, this has been dictated through political governance and a reluctance to address racial inequality politically. The 1990s draw several similarities and parallels with the present in regards to the heightened and partisan clamour for the British government to impose stricter legislations concerning border control and assert more hostile measures with regards to enforcing deportation in response to the perceived mass influx of immigrants infiltrating, draining, and exhausting state resources (Appiah, 2007; Woolley, 2011). The racialised stereotyping that often becomes masqueraded and conflated within the immigration and populist rhetoric defined for a generation a feeling of trespassing on the narrative of Britishness. The concept of trespassing, for many ethnic minorities within Britain, reflected a narrow and constrained lens of Britishness that was situated in Whiteness and cultural exclusion.

Racism is often conceptualised according to the historical context in which it is expressed (Solomos and Back, 1996). During this time, racism did not really differ across a national context; the capital city, London was attempting to endorse a hybridity of multi-culturalism that often resulted in the city being heralded as the example for the rest of Britain to follow. This differs when considering the host society and the specific cultural contexts that are infused within the dynamics of a local community (Bourne, 2001; St. Louis, 2007; Yuval-Davis, 1999). Alliances within particular communities can often reflect differing experiences of discrimination which entirely identify with a different type of racialised politics. Often, this could be reflected in the immediate and particular objectives of a far-right faction resulting in anti-racist movements having to be politically responsive and agile with regards to the variations of discrimination being projected. Based on this premise, singular forms of racism could be experienced, which became exclusive to particular ethnic minorities (Sivanandan, 1974; Warmington, 2014).

Understanding how contemporary political discourses in Britain impacted the 1990s is compelling because perspectives, personal reflections, and recollections essentially will be different depending on the diaspora that lived through this period based on the lived experience and subjective interpretations of the decade. Through this treatise, there has been a deliberate attempt to disrupt the notion that proliferated in the 1990s that somehow ethnic minorities were a threat to the unity and order of British society. Throughout the 1990s the new right portrayed Black and ethnic minority communities as a threat to the ideologies associated with Britishness. In essence, ethnic minorities were perceived as the enemy within, a threat towards the cultural and political views of a nation (Alleyne, 2007; Gilroy, 2000) – a somewhat fraught and misinformed disposition adopted by the far-right, but a clear indication that they rejected all forms of cultural integration and ethnic difference. The vehicle of the media was essential to the far-right in propelling this narrative by insinuating that the ever-increasing growth of the ethnic minority and migrant population threatened to jeopardise the White British population. The media became determined to portray ethnic minorities as a group that was difficult to integrate into British society. Deeply engrained within a dominant right-wing narrative, this rhetoric would continue to gain momentum and throughout the 1990s in attempting to reassert White supremacy and create new forms of racial subjectification.

Towards the end of the decade this reassertion attempted to portray Muslims as a threat to societal harmony and unity, while racialising other groups such as refugees and asylum seekers as posing a threat to fundamental British values (Ramdin, 1999). The embryonic stages of this ignorance at the time also purported threats to national security regarding cultural and religious unity. The fear projected was that of British identity being under threat and as customary the blame was laid squarely at the feet of ethnic minorities residing within Briton (Solomos, 2003).

Throughout the 1990s there was a denial regarding the preciousness of racism within Britain even after the murder of Stephen Lawrence. During this period there was still a residual denial which lingered from the late 1970s and 1980s that continued to deny the importance and centrality of racism within British society (Ramdin, 1987). The trivialisation of racism was further exacerbated because the institutional and societal tendency to deny a visceral hostility towards black people in Britain became increasingly more palpable, reinforcing racial discrimination. Situated within a nationalistic backdrop, the pervading ideology suggested that people preferred to live with their own kind and these ideals did not embrace differing types of cultural integration (Solomos, 2003). Of course this reaction signalled a subtle resistance provided by a section of society that did not want to live amongst individuals from different cultural and racial backgrounds (Gilroy, 1992). This prevailing narrative was propelled by Thatcher's conception which proffered that 'the moment a minority threatens to become a big one, people become frightened'. This comment fuelled and ignited a decisiveness that would come to define race relations within British society. Thatcher's inflammatory statement did much to foster and propel the rise of xenophobic debates within political commentary during the 1980s and 1990s. These comments also became the catalyst for a political party that became committed to defending the interests of the White British majority at the expense of ethnic minority communities within the UK.

It is daunting to observe this from the ethnic minority perspective as attempts to establish 'belonging' became compromised against a hostile environment facilitated by senior Parliamentarians of the time, who continuously perpetuated a rhetoric that situated ethnic minorities as 'space invaders' (Mirza, 1997; Warmington, 2013). This was hugely damaging for ethnic minorities attempting to establish cultural, economic, and professional footholds in what was increasingly becoming a more diversified Britain. The irrational fear associated with Thatcher's mantra of people becoming frightened as a minority continued to gather momentum resonated with a general resistance towards diversifying Britain which failed to acknowledge the positive impact and contribution of ethnic minorities within Britain professionally, economically, and socially. This context becomes important when considering a discourse that has always 'othered' ethnic minorities, even those who consider themselves as British by virtue of birthplace within the UK.

The positioning of ethnic minorities as 'space invaders' and not truly belonging has historically always been punctuated by a resistance towards globalisation and the rise in populism, thus creating a perfect storm for nationalists to reject the idea of an ethnically diverse Britain. Contextually, the concept of multi-culturalism has always been undermined by notions of cultural rejection (Gilroy, 2000). The potential for multi-culturalism during the early 1990s was undermined by a Conservative Government with little empathy for racial equality or dismantling a system that was structurally and inherently racist (Kundnani, 2007). This often placed ethnic minorities on the periphery of British society, with little agency to operate within the margins in an attempt to assimilate and integrate into British culture, an endeavour that became increasingly challenging due to a cultural, nationalistic resistance towards migrant workers.

Unpacking anti-racism during the 1990s

Throughout the 1990s, the term 'anti-racism' generated several commentaries which attempted to steer a fractured society towards the proverbial colour-blind promised land. Fundamentally, this honeyed landscape of equality promised a dialogue which would see the improvement of actual relationships between Black and White people within British society (Gilroy, 1992). Interestingly, there was a feeling that such interventions did not acknowledge the nuanced complexities of racism, its systemic reach, and its pernicious effect on ethnic minorities within British society. The racist institutions and the ideologies that accompanied them were a monument to the discriminatory terrain that permeated Britain at the time. Dismantling these discriminatory frameworks against a political machine that historically had not prioritised the needs of Black and ethnic minority people created a huge sense of vulnerability and uncertainty in attempting to navigate the racially discriminatory swamp that was Britain. Gilroy (1992) encapsulates this narrative by highlighting that, where the aims and objectives of Black struggles were made clear, they were both more extensive and more modest that the anti-racist label suggests. There is a context which speaks to these struggles being defined by the contextual relationship towards everyday experiences at the hands of their oppressors (Gilroy, 1992). There has and perhaps will always be a sophistication associated with racism because of how it persists through various incarnations within social structures. This has undoubtedly impacted upon resistance movements and interventions towards racism. The shifting paradigms concerning race and racism have been a continuous feature of racial politics and culture, resulting in the enforced adoption of a mental and cultural agility by ethnic minorities attempting to circumnavigate the ever-changing discriminatory landscape (Gilroy, 1992; Mirza, 1997).

Throughout the 1990s racism became an afterthought, culturally, politically, and socially. Attempts to neutralise racism became difficult without the elevated, priority status required politically to dismantle this particular type of discrimination or oppression. The 1990s facilitated the enduring narrative that the elimination of institutional racism among Parliamentarians within British society was never an essential political objective, except when illuminated by the embarrassing paucity of ethnic minority politicians with an organic investment and interest in race and racism. The burden of this unrequested plight was thrust upon their shoulders – such was the societal expectation at the time to elevate this issue.

The contexts that pervaded racism not only nationally but globally during the time provided a set of variables for racial subordination that shaped how racialised experiences were encountered, particularly when resistance movements began to gather momentum in the wake of the Brixton and Tottenham riots during the 1980s (Sivanandan, 1983). Throughout the 1990s we would observe a palpable and critical mass that became a proactive and spontaneous resistance to the institutionally racist system that effectively aided and abetted the unprovoked and racially motivated murder of Stephen Lawrence in the aftermath of this incident (Solomos, 2003; Yuval-Davis, 1999). The residual effects of these racialised experiences historically have been felt through many instruments of oppression, such as stereotyping, poor housing, unemployment, repatriation, limited access to professional services, and police brutality. As Gilroy (1992) states, ethnic minorities do not encounter racism in a vacuum that can be generalised or made abstract and its pernicious effect is felt through our societal institutions. The concrete manifestations of this oppression and the subjective interpretations aligned to this by those not experiencing this type of discrimination facilitated a complacency to ensue, which trivialized 'race' into an abstract conceptualisation which became undermined through social and political power relations as the far-right sought to defend all that represented Britannia, an ideal that did not include, embrace, or facilitate the idea of a multi-cultural Britain (Adi, 1995; Alexander, 1996; Hiro, 1973).

The various sites for which the racialised oppression was felt during the 1990s were understood as separate and external incidents that happened in 'blissful' isolation of what was otherwise a perfect and untarnished British utopia that warmly supported ethnic minorities. This melancholic narrative very much employed a reductionist approach towards racism which would reluctantly digest such experiences only if they were readily visible. Racist incidents often were subject to claims for accuracy regarding the motive for such discriminatory offences. For ethnic minorities, such proclamations became another instrument to perpetuate symbolic violence's and facilitate 'silencing' of racist incidents (Hiro, 1973; Warmington, 2009). This would remove the basic right even to cathartically verbalise such discriminatory experiences in public throughout the decade for fear of being accused of 'playing the race card', a prominent and fragile retort experienced when encountering a rear-guard action against racism (DiAngelo, 2018).

Perhaps on reflection, albeit a subjective one, New Labour attempted to make 'race' a meaningful factor by a acknowledging its existence as a societal and political problem that institutionally disadvantages Black and ethnic minorities (Gilroy, 1992). The complexity of racism and its centrality within the fabric of British society renders this a problem that can be characterised simply by the daily oppression encountered; the problem itself has continually proven to be too sophisticated for such constrained conceptions. What the MacPherson Report attempted to do – propelled by the unrelenting Lawrences, Doreen and Neville – was to reveal the complexity and perpetual effects of the underlying problems that ethnic minorities face as a result of a fundamentally racist British society (Yuval-Davis, 1999; Mirza, 1997).

There is a very true and accurate history that would suggest that ethnic minorities have been actively organising and mobilising themselves to defend against racism throughout British history. These struggles have notably developed a cohesion amongst Blacks and Whites seeking a more egalitarian society that embraces equity for all – and, perhaps most importantly within this context, Black liberation (Modood, 1994). The vocabulary that accompanied this resistance was often situated in the belief that we all have the capability to accept difference and live in a harmonious and neighbourly fashion. However, throughout the 1990s, the proliferation, expansion, and consolidation of political organisations from the extreme far-right also impacted, transformed, and arrested any traction made by the anti-racist movement as 'project fear' began to supersede the need for racial equality.

There were factions of British society that had built a hatred for ethnic difference over the several decades that preceded the 1990s. This 'cultural difference' and steadily increasing wave of migration remains to the present day an infiltration and assault on all things British. Consequently, there were individuals that were unwilling to accept new discourses, regarding what the term 'Britishness' could encompass and embody culturally. Increasingly, there was an appetite amongst nationalists to ethnically cleanse Britain, often through intimidating and unsavoury means which placed ethnic minority lives at risk. In a quest for Britain to become 'recognisable' again, racism was once again reincarnated with this particular model aiming now to penetrate the walls of Whitehall in an attempt to create a more symbolically violent and pernicious instrument through which to channel this disgruntlement and institutionally supported racial violence (Mirza, 1997; Parekh, 2000).

Step forward again into the fray the National Front (NF), a faction that could always be relied upon to violently peddle and mobilise xenophobia and racial hatred as they had done decades before resurfacing and rebranding again in the 1990s. Now defunct, the NF's unsuccessful attempt to rebrand as The British National Party (BNP) and become a more refined and polished political outfit in a quest to gain more mainstream support became futile in the face of anti-racist movements. Although their brand of politics gained like-minded, populist global admirers and comrades in the battle to oppose diversity and growing migration such factions remained on the fringes of British and global parliamentary politics. This fate was shared by other far-right fringe movements that embodied a similar illogical ignorance that positioned people of colour as inferior to White people, namely in South Africa, in the form of Afrikaner Resistance Movement, led by Afrikaner nationalist Eugene Terre'Blanche. His movement attempted to dismantle, through racial hatred, Mandela's Rainbow Nation and with it his vision for a New South Africa that attempted to endorse forgiveness as a tool to reconcile the oppressive White supremacist legacy of Apartheid.

The mainstream attention gleaned from these factions spoke to disenfranchised nationalists and as a result a collective swell of racialised, street-level harassment resurfaced compromising the safety of ethnic minorities. The historically fraught and fractured relationship that the police had with the Black community within Britain also meant that ethnic minorities had very little confidence in law enforcement to prioritise their safety and heed concerns regarding their general well-being as public citizens (Souhami, 2007). The anxiety heightened by the continual failure of the British judicial system to bring culprits of violent racist attacks to justice was palpable (Souhami, 2014). The Lawrence case continually reminded ethnic minorities how miscarriages of justice ensue when propped up by the beams of an institutionally racist structure. This definition of British neo-fascism allows for an adorning of yesteryear which heralds the British as all-conquering, with selective amnesias conveniently redirecting tainted histories through a very subjective rose-tinted lens. Such recollections provide a site for denial and a non-acceptance of the dangers of contemporary racism. The lethargy by the state that normally transpired during this period was reactive rather than proactive regarding the neutralising and extinguishing of neo-fascist groups such as the NF (Hall, 1998). As Gilroy (1992) states, in many cases neutralising such groups only occurs when this is viewed as a problem that could potentially threaten democracy through their participation within the electoral system. Despite a societal microscope on this group and a legacy of racial violence against Black individuals and communities, much of the abhorrent behaviour that supersedes these factions was made acceptable by a system that often chose not to engage in anti-racist movements or politics in favour of residing on safer ground, which resembled a more socialist anti-fascist politics (Hiro, 1973; Gilroy, 1992).

Principally, the main function of these anti-fascist committees was to operate as a self-conscious political formation providing a platform for anti-discriminatory dialogues. Although such dialogue was useful in illuminating struggles between the police and the Black community and issues concerning education and housing, the baton remained untaken by policy makers, some of whom one could argue benefit from a society that was and still is racially discriminatory and unequal. The momentum gained from these groups also provided a stimulus for global collaboration with other radical struggles, leading to ever-changing redefinitions of what the term anti-racism conveys to a global populace (Gilroy, 1992; Owusu, 2000).

The continuous challenging of Black liberation being made reducible to anti-racism, as Gilroy suggests, only sought to trivialise the gravity of racism as a term that could only really be enforced and conceptualised when dealing specifically with far-right, neo-fascist

groups. The populist weapons of the far-right were utilised to pernicious effect throughout the 1990s as this particular sect of society
gathered momentum, spearheaded by a racially flawed institutional
system that contributed to the positioning of ethnic minorities as a
'criminal threat'. These weapons were utilised to characterise and,
essentially, demonise people of colour in a somewhat successful
attempt to anecdotally create wide-ranging negative generalisations
about ethnic minorities that become engrained in the racist vernacular (Pilkington, 2003). These weapons essentially positioned 'Blacks'
as muggers, rapists, drug dealers, and gang affiliates and were further
reinforced by the positioning of ethnic minorities within the media
throughout the decade and beyond (Gilroy, 1992). This became an
effective deflection regarding the seemingly and culturally 'acceptable' racial hatred directed towards Black and ethnic minorities.

The convergence of this interest was seamless as once again
the topic of racism would temporarily dine at the table, only to be
rebuffed against a neo-fascist resistance that was now hanging its hat
on the rhetoric of 'Black crime' redefining criminal activity as solely
a 'Black endeavour'. Sadly, this became an inoperable societal cyst
that has generationally positioned Black people, especially Black
men, as deviant agents of criminality, a stereotype that has traversed
boundlessly throughout British history. The robustness and persistence of the far-right as an enduring effigy of discrimination sought
to strategically demonise Black people as 'less than' in comparison to
Whites. From both sides of the political divide, populist and anti-racist
movements will both coherently argue, of course based on subjective
interpretation, that they are fighting for the liberation of their people
(Alexander, 1996). Perhaps where anti-racist endeavour supersedes
populist exertion is that at the essence of the anti-racist struggle is a
desire for all human beings to be treated as equals, removed from an
ideology that positions ethnic minority people as an inferior species.

Throughout the 1990s the continuation and explosion of popular
nationalism was funnelled through music, media, and football, most
notably hooliganism and racism on the terraces, to name a few vehi-
cles through which this fascism transpired. As with all types of discrimination, although they are often oppressive, they can also become

an instrument for mobilising activism and political consciousness. The slippage that occurs when considering anti-racist movements during the 1990s normally situates this resistance as something that operated on the periphery of the political system. However successful, many of these movements in their varying guises had to adapt to a particular set of variables defined by the politics of the time and the circumstances within which racism pervaded. The commonality in these movements for liberation has been to illuminate and address the issue of Black disadvantage inside the institutional structures of British society (Woolley, 2011). Neo-fascism contests the idea of Black liberation, particularly within a British context; however, caution was required in applying and considering this particular discourse because although this has been an embodiment of contemporary racism, Gilroy (1992) argues that such conceptions enviably pull discussions of 'race' away from the centre of political culture, relocating this discourse on to the margins of political activity. The proliferation of equal opportunity policies has been necessary and, in some cases, useful in the formation of anti-racist initiatives. However, for people of colour to truly develop a sense of belonging that is not defined by cultural integration or migration with ethnic minorities from a similar background within Britain, there must be a political and societal framing that recognises the contribution that migrant populations have made to the cultural and economic infrastructure of Britain that moves away from racial subjectification, discrimination, oppression, and ignorance.

Mobilising a more tolerant, anti-racist Britain

Undoubtedly, the MacPherson Report was the key that unlocked the proverbial door to institutionalised racism within the UK, thereby bringing the discussion to the political and state table. The potential for greater social cohesion towards the end of the 1990s and beyond, as a result of the report represented a potential for counter-cultures and subcultures of Black Britain integrating with perhaps an emerging generation, exercising a maturity to become more tolerant and accepting of ethnic difference. The synchronic nature of culture can, when removed from the structural aspects of racism, provide opportunities for ethnic minorities to be uninhibited in their attempts to culturally integrate within Britain. Unpacking this potential within a contemporary British context requires an acknowledgment regarding instruments associated with 'race', nation, national culture, patriotism, and belonging.

Of course, within the guise of 'exclusion' and 'racialisation', these words acquired potent new meanings which became deeply implicated within the vernacular of racist discourse, particularly in the ways this became represented and mediated throughout the 1990s. These literary symbols and their intent hold various meanings, sometimes unsympathetically aligned with hypersensitivity or political correctness restricting free speech (Phillips, 2001). Throughout the decade there was a refusal to accept the political mediation of racism and the state's complicity in maintaining structural and institutional discrimination. However, the creation of solidarity from a sense of collective oppression became a source of strength, as many anti-racist movements reflected and continue to reflect. The characteristic of this collaborative resistance is a rejection of political behaviour that does not actively attempt to disrupt or dismantle institutional racism. This collective rejection became representative of an enthusiasm for direct political and social participation resulting in frontline action. Melucci (1980) conceptualises this most adeptly by recognising that Blacks have often struggled to escape the biologisation of their social and politically constructed subordination, resulting in having to be continually hyper-vigilant and cognisant of the terrain in which they reside as 'aliens' within British society.

Throughout the 1990s, anti-racist universality and the Black liberation movement would come to encapsulate varying potent meanings. The cultural locus associated with understanding race and racism was particularly intriguing for a generation of ethnic minority adolescents beginning to be forcefully introduced to the discriminatory terrain they would potentially reside in for their foreseeable futures within Britain. Race exhibits several social characteristics associated with penetrating the walls of a political system that during this time continued to victimise, marginalise, and oppress. As Gilroy asserts, penetrating the firmly embedded structures of the state concerning law and race are non-negotiable and, where they are not openly hostile to the institutions of the political system, its organisational forms fit only loosely and partially into it. The societal reconceptualisation of the Black individual has proven difficult for many to fathom; if anything, the 'racialised' rhetoric spun has been weaponised to sustain racist tropes and stereotypes. This sustains an imagery within Britain concerning race, in which the context of the ever-increasing ethnic minority population is directly associated with the imagery of Black criminality and lawlessness (Gilroy, 1992). Several anti-racist movements during the 1990s continuously attempted to dismantle the production of urban meanings which were situated as a constitutive of 'race', consequently positioning the city as a site for Black criminality and migrant settlers.

Contemporary definitions of race throughout the 1990s were continuously aligned through primitivism, often situating Black people with violent activity, particularly in inner-city areas. The context provided for 'race' throughout the decade simply connoted that wherever Black people resided, trouble and anarchy would swiftly follow (Alleyne, 2007). Again, the weaponisation of race came to mean that often, against this somewhat skewed theorisation, racial problems were rarely acknowledged and, if anything, were defined as a problem that was self-inflicted rather than an act of social conditioning that was inflicted by the state (Hiro, 1973; Farrar, 2004; Sivanandan, 1974). An important distinction to assert was that 'race' became a marker for the activity of urban social movements and their resistance towards political systems associated with the state. The subsequent suppression of race and racism throughout the decade created an ambivalence towards the issue which has allowed its perniciousness to sustain through several reincarnations, as a continuous tool of Whiteness that reduces racial discrimination to a political antagonism purely based on conjecture (Farrar, 2004; Gilroy, 1992; Kundnani, 2007). The desire to secure anti-racist polices was met with a rhetoric that suggested freedom of speech was being suppressed. Subsequently, throughout the 1990s this would allow for the continuation of a racist orthodoxy and autocracy which would permeate through Britain's social and political life. Gilroy encapsulates this narrative by explaining that racism has been defined as the product of Black and anti-racist zeal that is both destructive of democracy and subversive of order. Based on this premise, the right to be prejudiced was claimed as the birthright of the freeborn White Briton. Within this restrictive and tribal guise, only individuals from this ethnic category were able to articulate discourses of freedom, patriotism, and democracy, while contrastingly, anti-racism was associated with criminality, authoritarianism, statism, and censorship (Gilroy, 1992).

A British life: living together in harmony

The strong association between identity and territory is historically and culturally interwoven within the fabric of British society and individuals considered to infringe on this have done so in many cases by having to compromise their own physical, personal, mental, and economic well-being (Singh, 2000). There is a finite language that can be inclusive or equally exclusive that provides a commonality in experience, a solidarity that unifies individuals towards a shared ideal or vision. Community becomes a strong theme in subsequent local and national political organising around social-justice issues. It also is the binary that brings people together during times of euphoric, national celebration.

The initial emergence of a generation arising from the political quagmire of Thatcherism created a momentum that would encapsulate a seemingly new language that was inclusive of all members of society (Heffernan, 2001). As this narrative continued to become splintered, what we began to observe was the potential for the Cool Britannia years to integrate all members of society by celebrating the multi-faceted nature of British society and all of its inhabitants. Sadly, this period was utilised as a political football which actually became decisive, placing ethnic minorities on the periphery of what became an extremely and notably White phenomenon that ultimately extolled the virtues of populism and nationalism. Nationalism and populism became the order of the time, positioning the far-right as

lieutenants of a 'moral crusade' to rid Britain of 'foreigners' and keep
its shores exclusively White by any lawful or unlawful means necessary (Hiro, 1973; Alexander, 1996). The utilisation of these operant
tools of Whiteness would come unstuck against an anti-racist resistance that illuminated the long activist tradition and contribution of
Black and ethnic minorities to Britain and the importance of redefining and conceptualising the term 'Britishness' to encompass an ever-
changing multi-cultural society.

In many ways, Cool Britannia was complicit in widening the
chasm regarding race and racism and actually did little to eradicate
the problem; in many ways, it perpetuated and sustained a discourse
which very much excluded ethnic minorities based on a very racialised and narrow depiction of Britishness. However, there is a collective thankfulness on behalf of ethnic minorities from my generation
for the following: the dawn of New Labour in 1997 that provided
working class individuals with the opportunity to become socially
mobile and the dissemination of a report that would recognise the
institutional effects of structural racism on Black and ethnic minority people in Britain – albeit at the unnecessary and sad expense of
a promising young black architect from South London. For many
ethnic minorities continually enduring the sheer weight of racism
employed by the state and the complementary cultural exclusion
which accompanies this, these marginal gains will provide minimal
comfort. The reason being because the compromise has come at an
unquantifiable cost that has seen ethnic minority equality within
Britain banished to the political margins. Many continue to benefit
and profit from inequalities such as racial discrimination, fascism,
and xenophobia (Souhami, 2014). These discriminatory structures in
many ways provide a foothold upon which bastions of the far-right
can hinge their abhorrent views, sadly and perhaps unknowingly,
Cool Britannia became a vehicle for this, with the discriminatory
narrative becoming consumed within it. The Cool Britannia machine
was used to demonstrate a cohesive, inclusive, and tolerant Britain
during the 1990s; what this book has attempted to illustrate is that,
although this may be true for a largely White British populace, for
many ethnic minorities, this period of time represented something

entirely different. It represented a story of survival against the state during a time in which the instrument of racism was perhaps at its most effective in creating division and social disharmony within Britain through its major institutions (Hall, 1998; Warmington, 2014; Yuval-Davis, 1999).

That being said, there is a gravitational pull regarding this period throughout the 1990s, upon which reflections draw comparisons with the current national and political climate in relation to racism. Nearly 20 years on from the end of the 1990s, there is perhaps a sadness that many of those racialised discourses have in fact become more sophisticated as we begin to encounter a new generation of nationalists hell-bent on preserving the virtues of a 'racist' Britannia. These new sophisticated models include the Prevent Strategy, an intervention presented as a government counter-terrorism initiative which is in essence a form of racial ascribing and profiling. This strategy victimises ethnic minorities, particularly those from the Islamic faith. This more urbane form of racial discrimination, while sponsored and supported by the state, will always thrive, with its main function being to continually subjugate and disadvantage. The eternal wisdom behind stop and search will continue to be employed as a method by the state to incarcerate and criminalise young Black men. The blunt force trauma inflicted by this particular instrument has never subsided with time and continues to oppress and victimise young Black men in a way that, arguably, no other racialised instrument of the state within Britain can (Bygott, 1992; Souhami, 2007).

On reflection, what was taken from such a tumultuous period? The learning that ensued prepared at least a second generation of British-born ethnic minorities who were the children of migrants to understand what it meant to be a person of colour within a British society. Ethnic minorities are continuously hypervigilant of the institutional and structural racism and the cultures within our society that facilitate this hostile environment. People of colour, like their ancestors and socialist allies before them that mobilised Black liberation, recognise the potency of anti-racist resistance and the benefits that derive from all members of society being more tolerant of racial and ethnic difference (Alleyne, 2007; Farrar, 2004; Warmington, 2014).

The central tenet to this whistle-stop tour of the 1990s suggests that a present, modern-day reconceptualisation of 'Britishness' is long overdue and requires a reframing of this context that is not only more inclusive of ethnic minorities but secondly, acknowledges the continual dehumanisation of ethnic minorities and the hostile environment that they continually encounter. This acknowledgement becomes essential in establishing belonging and communal harmony that removes race and racism as a decisive mechanism that undermines the potential for social cohesion within multi-ethnic Britain.

The eternal optimist within yearns for a reconceptualisation of Britishness that incorporates equality and diversity whilst rejecting racism and embracing multi-culturalism as something to be celebrated. Imagining a more inclusive Britain is a socialist ideal and the promise for this resides within a narrative of hope. In reliving this particular period of time, ethnic minorities also endure the psychological and residual effects that have left them emotionally, mentally, and physically fatigued through having to continuously navigate institutional racism in all of its insidious forms. The continual navigation of racism by ethnic minorities within British society is testament to an enduring resilience and ability to survive in the eternal struggle to dismantle racial discrimination.

Conclusion

The interplay between Cool Britannia and multi-ethnic Britain is intriguing and occupies an interesting place in history when we attempt to discern how inclusive the period was for all British residents at the time of this phenomenon. Attempting to remove racism from the political margins to the centre of political discourse was and remains problematic. The marginalisation of ethnic minorities was the footnote to the Cool Britannia years. The state and its institutions were complicit in maintaining and sustaining racism; however, the attempt by anti-racism activists to identity and shape a new lexicon that endorsed cultural diversity as a vehicle for multi-culturalism is to be applauded. Anti-racist endeavour has always been the product of a double kind of consciousness that requires a continuous shifting between paradigms which traverse many inequitable terrains, moving between the margins and the centre, alienation and belonging, alignment and critique (Warmington, 2014).

In attempting to present a synopsis of the 1990s through a slightly different lens, this book has attempted to draw upon a myriad of examples, contexts, and auto-ethnographies to position the complexity of discrimination and cultural exclusion in understanding how Britain operated as a fundamentally institutionally racist society throughout the decade. This book is but one attempt to portray a narrative that recognises the presence of ethnic minorities during that period. This treatise also acknowledges the enduring and pernicious nature of racism when we as a British society choose to reject equality in favour of inequality, and endorse segregation rather than integration.

Maybe I will never be . . . All the things that I wanna be . . . Now is not the time to cry . . . Now's the time to find out why, I think you're the same as me . . . We see things they'll never see.

('Live Forever', Oasis, 1994)

References

Adi, H. (1995) *The History of African and Caribbean Communities in Britain*. Hove: Wayland.

Alexander, C. (1996) *The Art of Being Black: The Creation of Black British Youth Identities*. Oxford: Clarendon Press.

Alleyne, B. (2002) *Radicals Against Race: Black Activism and Culture Politics*. Oxford: Berg.

Alleyne, B. (2007) 'Anti-racist cultural politics in post-imperial Britain: The New Beacon Circle', in R. Day, G. De Peuter and M. Cote (eds.), *Utopian Pedagogy: Racial Experiments Against Neoliberal Globalization*, Toronto: University of Toronto Press, pp. 207–226.

Anderson, B. (1983) *In the Tracks of Historical Materialism*. London: Verso.

Anthias, F., & Yuval-Davis, N. (1983) 'Contextualizing feminism: Ethnic, gender and class divisions', *Feminist Review*, 15: 62–75.

Anthias, F., & Yuval-Davis, N. (1992) *Racialized Boundaries: Race, Nation, Gender, Colour and Class and the Anti-racist Struggle*. London: Routledge.

Appiah, K. A. (2007) *Cosmopolitanism: Ethics in a World of Strangers*. New York: Norton.

Ball, S. (2008) *The Education Debate: Policy and Politics in the Twenty-first Century*. Bristol: Policy Press.

Banton, M. (1977) *The Idea of Race*. London: Tavistock.

Bell, D. (1992) *Faces at the Bottom of the Well: The Permanence of Racism*. New York: Basic Books.

Bhabha, H. (1994) *The Location of Culture*. London: Routledge.

Bhopal, K., & Maylor, U. (eds.) (2014) *Educational Inequalities: Difference and Diversity in Schools and Higher Education*. London: Routledge.

Bloch, A., & Solomos, J. (2010) *Race and Ethnicity in the 21st Century*. London: Palgrave Macmillan.

Bourne, J. (2001) 'The life and times of institutional racism', *Race & Class*, 43 (2): 7–22.

Brah, A. (1996) *Cartographies of Diaspora, Contesting Identities*. London; New York: Routledge.

Bygott, D. (1992) *Black and British*. Oxford: Oxford University Press.

DiAngelo, R. (2018) *White Fragility: Why It's So Hard for White People to Talk About Racism*. Boston, MA: Beacon Press.

Driver, S., & Martell, L. (2006) *New Labour*. Cambridge: Polity.

Farrar, M. (2004) 'Social movements and the struggle over race', in M. Todd and G. Taylor (eds.), *Democracy and Participation: Protest and New Social Movements*. London: Merlin Press.

Gillborn, D., & Mirza, H. S. (2001) *Educational Inequality: Mapping Race, Class and Gender*. London: Ofsted.

Gilroy, P. (1987) *Ain't no Black in the Union Jack*. Abingdon: Routledge.

Gilroy, P. (1992) *There Ain't No Black in the Union Jack*. London: Routledge.

Gilroy, P. (1993) *The Black Atlantic: Modernity and Double Consciousness*. London: Verso.

Gilroy, P. (2000) *Against Race: Imagining Political Culture Beyond the Colour Line*. Cambridge, MA: Harvard University Press.

Grasso, M. (2016) *Generations, Political Participation and Social Change in Western Europe*. London: Routledge.

Hall, S. (1990) 'Cultural identity and diaspora', in J. Rutherford (ed.), *Identity: Community, Culture, Difference*. London: Lawrence and Wishart, pp. 222–237.

Hall, S. (1998) 'Aspirations and attitude: Reflections on Black Britain in the nineties', Frontiers/Backyards, special issue of *New Formations*, 33: 38–46.

Harris, J. (2004) *Britpop! Cool Britannia and the Spectacular Demise of English Rock*. London: Da Capo Press.

Heffernan, R. (2001) *New Labour and Thatcherism: Political Change in Britain*. Basingstoke: Palgrave Macmillan.

Heffernan, R., Hay, C., Russell, M., & Cowley, P. (eds.) (2016) *Developments in British Politics Ten*. London: Macmillan Education.

Heppell, T. (2014) *The Tories*. London: Bloomsbury.

Hindmoor, A. (2004) *New Labour at the Centre: Constructing Political Space*. Oxford: Oxford University Press.

Hiro, D. (1972) *Black British, White British: A History of Race Relations in Britain*. London: Grafton.

Hiro, D. (1973) *Black British, White British: A History of Race Relations in Britain*. London: Graffton.

Hitchens, C. (2004) *Blood, Class, and Empire: The Enduring Anglo-American Relationship*. New York: Nation Books.

HMSO (1976) *Select Committee on Race Relations and Immigration Session 1975–1976: The West Indian Community*. London: Metropolitan Police Evidence.

Housee, S. (2012) 'What's the point? Antiracism and students' voice against Islamophobia', *Race, Ethnicity and Education*, 15 (1): 101–120.

Hunte, J. (1965) *Nigger Hunting in England?* London: West Indian Standing Conference.

Keith, M. (1993) *Race, Riots and Policing: Lore and Disorder in Multiracist Society*. London: UCL Press.

Kenny, M. (2015) 'The return of Englishness' in British political structure: The end of the Unions', *Journal of Common Market Studies*, 53 (1): 35–51.

Kundnani, A. (2007) *The End of Tolerance: Racism in 21st Century Britain*. London: Pluto.

Kymlicka, W. (1996) *Multicultural Citizenship: A Liberal Theory of Minority Rights*. Oxford: Oxford University Press.

Lammy, D. (2011) *Out of the Ashes: Britain the Riots*. London: Guardian Books.

Leonardo, Z. (2005) Through the multicultural glass: Althusser, ideology and race relations in post-civil rights America, *Policy Futures in Education*, 3 (4): 400–412.

Macpherson, W./Home Office (1999) *The Stephen Lawrence Inquiry: Report of an Inquiry by Sir William Macpherson*. London: HMSO.

Marable, M. (1997) 'Rethinking black liberation: Towards a new protest paradigm', *Race and Class*, 38 (4): 1–13.

Melucci, A. (1980) 'The new social movements: A theoretical approach', *Social Science Information*, 19: 2–17.

Miles, R. (1982) *Racism and Migrant Labour*. London: Routledge and Kegan Paul.

Miles, R. (1989) *Racism*. London: Routledge.

Mirza, H. S. (1997) *Black British Feminism: A Reader*. Abingdon: Routledge.

Modood, T. (1992) *Not Easy Being British: Colour, Culture and Citizenship*. London: Runnymede/Trentham.

Modood, T. (1994) 'Political blackness and British Asians', *Sociology*, 28 (4): 859–876.

Modood, T. (2007) *Multiculturalism: A Civic Idea*. Cambridge: Polity Press.

Modood, T., & Acland, T. (eds.) (1998) *Race and Higher Education: Experiences, Challenges and Policy Implications*. London: Policy Studies Institute.

Neal, S. (2003) 'The Scarman report, the Macpherson report and the media: How newspapers respond to race-centred social policy interventions', *Journal of Social Policy*, 32 (1): 55–74.

Owusu, K. (ed.) (2000) *Black British Culture and Society: A Text Reader.* London: Routledge.

Parekh, B. (2000) *The Future of Multi-Ethnic Britain: Report of the Commission on the Future of Multi-Ethnic Britain.* London: Profile.

Parekh, B. (2006) *Rethinking Multiculturalism: Cultural Diversity and Political Theory, 2nd Edition.* Basingstoke: Palgrave Macmillan.

Phillips, M. (2001) *London Crossings: A Biography of Black Britain.* London: HarperCollins.

Phillips, M., & Phillips, T. (1999) *Windrush: The Irresistible Rise of Multiracial Britain.* London: HarperCollins.

Pilkington, A. (2003) *Racial Disadvantage and Ethnic Diversity in Britain.* Basingstoke: Palgrave Macmillan.

Pilkington, A. (2013) The interacting dynamics of institutional racism in higher education. *Race Ethnicity and Education,* 16 (2): 225–245.

Preston, J. (2010) 'Concrete and abstract racial domination', *Power and Education,* 2 (2): 115–125.

Ramdin, R. (1987) *Reimaging Britain: 500 Years of Black and Asian History.* London: Pluto.

Ramdin, R (1999) *Reimaging Britain: 500 Years of Black Working Class in Britain.* London: Pluto.

Rex, J., & Tomlinson, S. (1979) *Colonial Immigrants in a British City: A Class Analysis.* London: Routledge.

Robinson, C. (1983) *Black Marxism: The Making of the Black Radical Tradition.* London: Zed.

Rose, E., & Deakin, N. (1969) *Colour and Citizenship: A Report on British Race Relations.* Oxford: Oxford University Press.

Rush, A. S. (2002) 'Imperial identity in colonial minds: Harold Moody and the League of Coloured Peoples 1931–1950', *Twentieth Century British History,* 13 (4): 356–383.

Sahgal, G., & Yuval-Davis, N. (eds.) (1992) *Refusing Holy Orders.* London: Virago.

Scarman, Lord G. (1982) *The Scarman Report: The Brixton Disorders 10th-12th April 1981.* Harmondsworth: Pelican.

Searle, C. (1973) *The Forsaken Lover: White Words and Black People.* Harmondsworth: Penguin.

Shukra, K. (1998) *The Changing Pattern of Black Politics in Britain.* London: Pluto.

Singh, G. (2000) 'The concept and context of institutional racism', in A. Marlow and B. Loveday (eds.), *After Macpherson: Policing After the Stephen Lawrence Inquiry.* Lyme Regis: Russell House, pp. 29–40.

Sivanandan, A. (1974) *Race and Resistance: The IRR Story.* London: Race Today.

Sivanandan, A. (1982) *A Different Hunger: Writing on Black Resistance.* London: Pluto.

Sivanandan, A. (1983) 'Challenging racism: Strategies for the 80s', *Race and Class*, 25 (2): 1–11.

Sivanandan, A. (2006) 'Attacks on multicultural Britain pave the way for enforced assimilation', *Guardian*, 14 April 2019, p. 32.

Solomos, J. (2003) *Race and Racism in Britain, 3rd Edition.* Basingstoke: Palgrave Macmillan.

Solomos, J., & Back, L. (1996) *Racism and Society.* Basingstoke: Palgrave Macmillan.

Song, M. (2003) *Choosing Ethnic Identity.* Cambridge: Polity Press.

Souhami, A. (2007) 'Understanding institutional racism: The Stephen Lawrence inquiry and the police service reaction', in M. Rowe (ed.), *Policing Beyond Macpherson.* Cullompton: Willan, pp. 66–87.

Souhami, A. (2014) 'Institutional racism and police reform: An empirical critique', *Policing and Society*, 24 (1): 1–21.

St. Louis, B. (2007) *Rethinking Race, Politics, and Poetics: C.L.R. James' Critique of Modernity.* London: Routledge.

Tomlinson, S. (2008) *Race and Education: Policy and Politics in Britain.* Maidenhead: Open University Press.

Tonry, M. (2004) *Punishment and Politics: Evidence and Emulation in English Crime Control Policy.* Cullompton: Willan.

Warmington, P. (2009) 'Taking race out of scare quotes: Race conscious social analysis in an ostensibly post-racial world', *Race Ethnicity and Education*, 12 (3): 281–296.

Warmington, P. (2013) 'Agents of critical hope: Black British narratives', in V. Bozalek, B. Leibowitz, R. Carolissen and M. Boler (eds.), *Discerning Critical Hope in Educational Practices.* London: Routledge.

Warmington, P. (2014) *Black British Intellectuals and Education: Multiculturalism's Hidden History.* London; New York: Routledge.

Woolley, S. (2011) 'We can indulge this nostalgia: Racism today is subtle and complex', *Guardian*, 15 April 2019. Online: www.theguardian.com/commentisfree/2011/aug/15/modern-racism-complex-sophisticated-approach

Yuval-Davis, N. (1994) Women, ethnicity and empowerment, *Feminism & Psychology*, 4 (1): 179–197.

Yuval-Davis, N. (1999) 'Institutional racism, cultural diversity and citizenship: Some reflections on reading the Stephen Lawrence inquiry report', *Sociological Research Online*, 4 (1): 1–9.

Index